To Dad
here's to many laughs!
Joe and Maggie

"GODFREY DANIELS!"

Verbal and Visual Gems from the Short Films of W.C. Fields

edited by
Richard J. Anobile

Introduction by Raymond Rohauer

A DARIEN HOUSE BOOK

DISTRIBUTED BY CROWN PUBLISHERS, INC.
NEW YORK, NEW YORK

A DARIEN HOUSE BOOK

The following films
are copyrighted by and owned by Raymond Rohauer
and used by special arrangement with him. The
films are registered in the Copyright Office of
The Library of Congress, Washington, D.C. as follows:

THE BARBER SHOP (1933) © DU 84159, R 273594
THE DENTIST (1932) © DU 83896, LP 2605
THE FATAL GLASS OF BEER (1932) © DU 84160
THE GOLF SPECIALIST (1930) © DU 84162
THE PHARMACIST (1933) © DU 84161, R 271988
POOL SHARKS (1915) © MP 25501
DOWN MEMORY LANE (1949) © LP 2605 , DU 20535

DISTRIBUTED BY:
CROWN PUBLISHERS, INC.
419 PARK AVENUE SOUTH
NEW YORK, NEW YORK 10016

ISBN 0-517-520-346

Library of Congress Catalogue Card Number: 75-4263
Printed in the United States of America

THE SHORT FILMS OF W.C. FIELDS are available for distribution through
Mr. Raymond Rohauer, 44 West 62nd Street, New York City 10023.

Preface

My earlier *A Flask of Fields* presented sequences from many of the feature films starring W.C. Fields. This volume concentrates on four short films: *The Dentist* (1932), *The Fatal Glass of Beer* (1932) *The Pharmacist* (1933), and *The Barber Shop* (1933). These do not comprise the entire output of shorts starring Fields, but in my estimation they are the cream.

These are his last four short films. Fields was given total control.

Under the aegis of Mack Sennett, he was able to produce shorts which forever set the pattern for his character: the nagging wives, the obnoxious children, the empty boasts and human cruelty are all here. This Fields is undistilled. He had yet to get into the Paramount and Universal Studio movie mills; he didn't have to conform to studio executives and their codes.

Fields and his art are discussed on the following pages by historian and collector Raymond Rohauer. My interest in film classics was fired by Raymond who gave me a solid foundation in the field when I assisted him during his tenure as Film Curator of the Gallery of Modern Art in New York City.

Let me just point out that what you have here are reconstructions of scenes. Unlike my *Film Classics Library*, this comedy series does not present films in their entirety.

There are over 800 frame blowups here taken directly from original material. These blowups are coupled with every word of dialogue for each scene and it is my hope that the sequences will work for you in this form. I selected the scenes based upon my own feelings about the material coupled with how well they work in book format. I would dearly have loved to have included scenes from *The Golf Specialist* (1930), but I found that I couldn't get it to work within the confines of this volume. Rather than take up over half of this book with such a sequence, I decided it would be better to compile more scenes from the four shorts included here.

You will also notice what some persons consider a rather risque sequence within the section on *The Dentist*. Aside from being possibly suggestive, it is quite cruel; in fact, I doubt if I've ever seen a more cruel Fields. The sequence was censored for many years and has been restored only recently. I include it here as a matter of historical record and remind those who might blush that whatever conclusions they draw are strictly in their heads.

Richard J. Anobile
New York City
March, 1975

W.C. Fields

by
Raymond Rohauer

HIS CAREER

William Claude Dukinfield—better known as W.C. Fields—detested the City of Brotherly Love with an indecent passion dating back to 1890.

Born April 9, 1879 in Philadelphia, he ran away from home at age 11 after a fight with his autocratic father, and began living quite literally off the streets, first as a newspaper hawker, subsequently as a juggler. Even at this early age, his bizarre sense of humor asserted itself: instead of shouting out the headlines as did the other newsboys, young Dukinfield would tantalize passers-by with obscure items from one of the inside pages.

Clearly, Philadelphia would not do. Fifty years later, by now a national radio star, he would observe, "Last week, I went to Philadelphia, but it was closed." Earlier, in the 1920's, when the editors of *Vanity Fair* asked a number of prominent people what they'd like for an epitaph, Fields replied, "On the whole, I'd rather be in Philadelphia." And in *My Little Chickadee*, playing a condemned man about to be hung, he is asked for his last request. "I'd like to see Paris," he muses, but seeing the hostile reaction on the faces of his executioners, he adds hastily, "...but Philadelphia will do."

Three years after running away from home, having taught himself juggling, Fields went professional. But the 14-year-old—who was to spend the next 20 years performing all over the world—didn't just juggle oranges: he juggled objects none of his fellow performers would dare handle, such as cigar boxes. And he played it not for virtuosity but for laughs.

Long after he left juggling for the films, he would slip in touches of his performing art—often to the fury of his directors who questioned the suitability of a juggling scene where none was called for.

Yet it was juggling and other on-stage vaudeville tricks that provided Fields with the basis for the magnificent stage character he was to develop, and perfect, in his later years.

In those early days, the traveling vaudevillian was low man on the social totem-pole, and thus easy prey for rapacious swindlers and larcenous petty officials. Where his colleagues would have to tolerate this seamy aspect of their lives offstage, Fields managed to turn each grudge into a priceless asset—a mordantly-stinging sense of satire. Consider how many times in his later films he is seen venting his spleen against insurance agents, stock swindlers, embezzling stage managers, writ-writing sheriffs, greedy relatives, pompous employers and just about anyone else walking who ever crossed his path. (As he intoned to Mae West in *My Little Chickadee*, "the country is fraught with marauders"—as capsule a commentary on the human condition as Fields could muster.)

Yet, he certainly did not exempt himself from such company. Fields always presented himself on screen as a braggart and a windbag, a coward and a schemer—and perpetually in need of or in search for a drink. And if he happened to have emerged from his perennial fight with a hostile world, then surely it was by accident.

Still, the audience sympathized with him, not because of any heroic antics but because he was invariably surrounded by such repulsive villains and sheer imbeciles that his own vices appeared, if not necessarily endearing, at least comparatively acceptable.

He spared no one, not even his former wife, nor son Claude (from whom he was estranged throughout his entire life). His screen wives were usually nagging shrews, mindless social climbers and greedy harridans. Claude did not simply emerge as the ne'er-do-well son but as son-in-law, nephew, and other gradations of familial oaf and insolent sponger. And just to make sure *he* would know who was being depicted, the characters were almost always named "Claude."

It all began, on stage, in 1905, when he took a small speaking part in a London stage production, graduating several years later back in America as a headliner in seven editions of the famous Ziegfeld Follies, one each of George White's Scandals and Earl Carroll's Vanities. As a vaudevillian, Fields' specialties were sketches involving golf or pool, for which he had a number of props of his own making.

The big break came in 1923, when producer Philip Goodman, casting his musical comedy *Poppy,* offered Fields the part of Eustace McGargle. This McGargle was a confidence man who would try every nefarious scheme known to man, but who—as a latter-day Robin Hood—would redeem himself by spending his "take" to better the life of his adopted daughter.

It was inspired casting, for this McGargle, like Fields, was a man who could deal out as many blows as society bestowed on him, and who, not so incidentally, would ad lib a few innuendos reflecting his own jaundiced feelings about society that were clearly not in any script. It was largely due to Fields' masterful performance that the play kept running on Broadway for two years. He became so identified as McGargle that, contrary to prevailing practices, he portrayed McGargle in both the 1925 and 1936 screen versions of the play. What made this feat so unusual was that most memorable stage portrayals at the time were recreated on screen by players other than the original actors.

Not surprisingly, Fields knew he had hit a gold mine with McGargle, and kept mining this mother lode for the rest of his career. Fields simply used the skeleton of McGargle under various disguises, adding a little more or a little less vitriol as the plot demanded. From the film producers' viewpoint as well, this turned out to be a most serviceable arrangement: Fields' patently fraudulent and unctuous posture on screen, as well as his pompously arcane language and his outrageous mendacity made them wealthy—and delight us to this very day.

Fields' appearance in the screen-version of *Poppy* was not his first film; actually, he had tried the fledgling film industry as early as 1915, appearing in several silent comedy shorts for The Gaumont Company, of which only one—*Pool Sharks*—is preserved. And in 1924, he had done a walk-on as a drunken British sergeant in one of the films that William Randolph Hearst had financed for his protegee, Marion Davies.

But then came *Poppy*—and a Paramount contract that kept him busy for the rest of the '20's in the Long Island City studios in New York. It was a convenient arrangement as it allowed him to fulfill his film obligations while also appearing on stage for Flo Ziegfeld.

What we remember most today about Fields was his whining voice. Yet, the mere fact that Fields could successfully make nine silent feature films in four years shows just how successful a pantomimist he really was. Even without voice, Fields' presence in these early films was so powerful that he emerges triumphant over banal scripts and incompetent fellow players.

Poppy—or as the 1925 film was titled, *Sally of the Sawdust*—is historically important in that it brought together Fields and a director not known for comedy, D.W. Griffith. This odd couple produced a symbiotic film—one that enabled Fields to sneak in a few of his juggling tricks and *sotto-voced* stage tricks while allowing Griffith to do his things, such as the inevitable melodramatic prologue and a tightly-edited chase climax.

When sound arrived, so did Fields. In 1930, he brought to the screen one of his favorite golf routines from the Follies, and following RKO's *The Golf Specialist* came the 1931 Warner Brothers film operetta, *Her Majesty Love*. Despite his late entry in that film, he completely dominates the screen from that point on to the end credits.

That year (1931) he left the East for Hollywood for good, appearing in no fewer than 42 films (including guest shots) for a succession of studios—first Paramount, then Universal and United Artists. Among some of these roles were those of Humpty Dumpty in the 1933 *Alice in Wonderland* and of Mr. Micawber in the 1935 *David Copperfield*. Yet, we remember Fields primarily for some 20 sound films.

And for his legendary radio battles with Edgar Bergen's dummy "Charlie McCarthy" during the last few years of his life. And before he died, in 1946, Fields also recorded two hilarious monologues—"The Temperance Lecture" and "The Day W.C. Fields Drank a Glass of Water." Ironically, when originally issued on four 78 rpm shellac records, they were barely profitable. But reissued 25 years later on LP, it became #41 in national sales—an astonishingly posthumous feat, considering that these skits had been around for at least ten years on a half a dozen fly-by-night or bootleg labels.

When he breathed his last breath on Christmas Day of 1946—no doubt well laced with what he would have surely called *spiritus frumenti*—he was already assured a comfortable spot in Hollywood's Pantheon. His offbeat, irreverent and trenchant humor led a few close associates to issue a eulogy in which they hailed him as the most original American humorist since Mark Twain.

Whether true or simply West Coast hyperbole really depends on the eye and ear of the beholder. No one will quarrel with the verdict that W.C. Fields was perhaps the 20th century's most eccentric comic, his unorthodoxy exceeded only by his keen self-sense of outrageous individuality.

HIS ART

A comedian has several ways to present his craft: he can look funny, he can act funny, he can say funny things, and if he is a real professional, he can say things funny.

Fields, of course, using all of these ways was every inch a professional. His appearance was always a bit on the pompous side, emphasizing middle-class ostentation. He moved and acted in a funny way, using a number of bits of business inherited from his stage days—getting entangled with a sticky piece of paper, forever losing his hat on the tip of the upraised cane, getting sprinkled by a watering can and blaming an innocent dog, etc. The things he said were often funny lines, most of them written by himself, others contributed by other writers.

Above all, however, Fields had a keen professional ear for sounds. He put things in a way that was uniquely his own. Part of the credit for this was due to his early background. Having to live on his own, largely by his own wits, his was an education picked up as he went along. His language was the product of the streets combined with curiously esoteric reading habits. Add to this his natural attraction to the bizarre expression of sound, and what came out was a highly original language, full of old-fashioned flowery terms of endearment, strange exclamations and euphonious tongue twisters. Listen to the sound-tracks of his films:

He calls his women "my slender reed," "my little plum," or "my Rocky Mountain canary." He enriches his dialogue with exaggerated Victorian politeness, such as "Pardon my redundancy." He will correctly use recondite words like "dulcimer," "ipecac," "kumquat," "mukluk," "assagai," or "an arboreal dell." Yet in the next breath, without batting an eyelash or

changing his somnolent expression, he will make up an outrageous monstrosity, like the fictional disease "mogo-on-the-gogogo." Next might come a self-originated expletive like "Godfrey Daniels!" or "Mother-of-Pearl!" And for good measure, he will throw in a nonsensical adage like "The big city ain't no place for a young girl, but pretty men go there!"

His quirk for the odd sounding word permeates all his dialogue. His scripts are full of names like Ouliotta Hemoglobin, Abigail Twirlbaffing, Hermisilio Brunch, Filthy McNasty, J. Pinkerton Snoopington, Oglethorpe P. Bushmaster, and Senor Guillermo McKinley, the half-breed from Guatemala. Fields' biographer, Robert Lewis Taylor, claimed that most of them were names of real people whom Fields had met in his travels, and whose sound attracted him for one reason or another.

While that is difficult to believe, or check, it is easy to confirm that the names of exotic places which he uses whenever he launches one of his shamelessly mendacious adventure tales are invariably real. Uncannily, he finds the oddest ones: Lake Titicaca, Darjeeling or Afghanistan. Back home, he lovingly dwells on the harmonics of Punxsutawney, Pennsylvania, Homosassa, Florida or Lompoc, California.

In *The Golf Specialist*, he wraps his tongue around the term "mashie niblick" with unabashed delight, several times. Becoming irritated with his caddy, he informs him of his intention to hit him on the head with the club, "I shall smite you on the sconce with this truncheon."

Give him a word like "Beelzebub," and he will work it into a script, whether it belongs there or not. Or "velocipede," which he uses in at least two films. (Yet, with typical perversity, he does not mention it in the one in which he is briefly seen riding one.)

The very names of his films confirm that he had much to say about the subject. One can hardly imagine studio executives agreeing without a fight to naming one of his films *The Man on the Flying Trapeze* (1935) when it had nothing remotely to do with the subject. The phrase *"Never Give a Sucker an Even Break"* does not appear in the 1941 Fields film of that name, but it does appear in *Poppy* (1936). He just seems to have liked certain phrases, like "It's the old Army game," or "You can't cheat an honest man," and insisted on them being catchy enough to use as titles, regardless of subject matter.

There are basically two types of statements that Fields could make funnier than anyone. In the first category are those prompted by his cantankerous, suspicious, chronically disgruntled outlook on the world which was Fields himself, rather than the screen character he was supposed to represent. They usually attack one sacred cow or another:

Motherhood: "I'd never hit a woman, not even my mother!"

Children: "They are very good—with mustard! Yes, I like children. Girl children. About eighteen or twenty."

Drinking: "I never drink anything stronger than gin before breakfast."

Mothers-in-law: "It is hard to lose a mother-in-law. Almost impossible."

The screen Fields comes off as an individual bent on his own pursuits, which the society about him does not condone. He is continually at odds with the law, with relatives, creditors and authorities, and fends them off with artifice and cunning.

If today's youth feel alienated, they have nothing on Fields. In *The Bank Dick*, he comes home after accidentally (of course) becoming the town hero. His termagant of a wife, playing hostess to some of her slatternly friends, ignores his timid statement of how he caught the robber and tells him sternly to take off his hat. "They gave me a reward," he tries again. "How dare you smoke in here?" raves the wife, completely ignoring what he says. Even later, as the scene switches to a mansion he apparently bought her, she hustles him out of the house when she is expecting her friends. Throughout the picture, his little daughter keeps throwing rocks at him and kicking him in the shins at unguarded moments; she also loudly proclaims to company that "father is drunk again," and other endearments.

It should be remembered that Fields was doing this type of comedy at a time when the movies depicted everything as sweetness and light. Shirley Temple and Andy Hardy were the queen and king of Hollywood. His satire, in contrast with this pablum, has a mordant pungency which was then quite daring, and which has not lost its flavor even now. In fact, it has the same quality that Fields himself ascribed to sex: "There may be other things that are better, and still others that are worse—but there is nothing quite like it."

Much has been said on the subject of the anti-hero, which is often quoted as if it were an invention of the current nihilistic culture. Yet Fields always was the protagonist who refused to be liked, remained unregenerate throughout the picture, and triumphed undeservedly and often without any effort on his part.

He never asked for audience sympathy, thus going against one of the sacred maxims of show business. He was neither pure and heroic, nor charming and slightly dumb (so that the audience could feel superior to him)—the two sure ways to achieve such sympathy. He is not particularly likable, and he doesn't curry favor with the audience by being humble. As he sits in with a few card sharks, a stranger asks if this is a game of chance. "Not the way I play it, no," he intones, so that we need not feel sorry for him when it turns out he is playing with crooks even worse than he and winds up fleeced.

No wonder Fields remains today one of the giants of entertainment, capable of bridging the generation gap effortlessly. And like all giants of the film, he rises above his times and his material, reaching out from the silver screen to strike responsive chords in anyone attuned to his unique, irreverent humor.

Virginity: "A virgin is a girl of about four. Very ugly."

As can be seen from these examples, the Fields way of delivering such a statement is to make first an already strong declaration, come to a stop, and then top it with a really outrageous clincher.

The same heightening of the audacity of his words can be found in the other category of sayings, those prompted by the alleged braggadocio of the character he portrays. He will utter a brazen lie, then embellish it, and finally carry it to an unheard-of absurdity. Thus, in *The Bank Dick* (1940), having made sure the audience has witnessed his cowardice, he boasts how he overcame a bank robber: "The guy pulled a knife on me, this long—it was really a dagger—a veritable assagai!!" It is typical of Fields that in this last topper, he doesn't care that most of his audience might have trouble understanding the little used word for an African spear. He has satisfied himself, and that's enough. Probably for the same reason, many of his incomparable asides are muttered almost unintelligibly, as if to suggest that it is our loss if we miss them, not his.

A mere inflection is enough for Fields to convey a meaning fraught with innuendo—and yet safe from the censor. A society lady asks him how his ping-pong is. "Fine—how's yours?" he inquires, in a way that suggests all sorts of lewd implications.

It is not surprising that W.C. Fields' humor has been revived by a new generation. First of all, it is so oddball that it is timeless, and therefore topical obsolescence does not affect it as much as it does the material of more down-to-earth comedians. It is something of an acquired taste—but one that is easily acquired, especially by a generation that rejects the values of the established order, since that is exactly what Fields had been doing way back then.

ACKNOWLEDGMENTS

I would like to take this opportunity to thank those individuals whose cooperation helped to make this book possible.

The rights to produce "Godfrey Daniels!" were granted by Mr. Raymond Rohauer. Raymond is a dedicated film historian who has contributed a great deal to the preservation of many film classics.

Alyne Model, George Norris and Jan Kohn of Riverside Film Associates once again handled all technical aspects of this project. They accurately transferred my frame selections to the negative materials which were then blown by the Vita Print Corp. of New York under the watchful eye of Saul Jaffe.

Harry Chester Associates was responsible for the design and layout of this book and their skill and imagination helped make my job easier. And Helen Garfinkle at Darien House worked hard to see that my wires didn't get crossed.

Richard J. Anobile

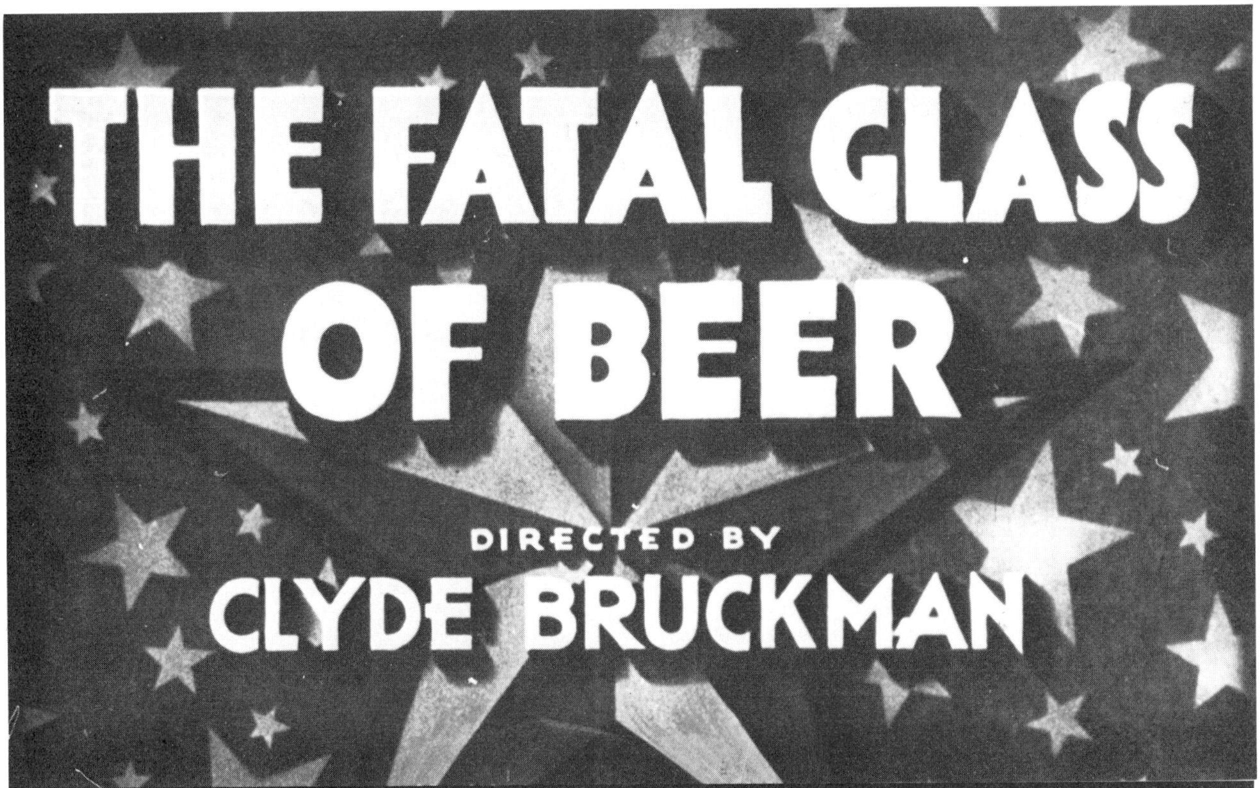
THE FATAL GLASS
OF BEER
DIRECTED BY
CLYDE BRUCKMAN

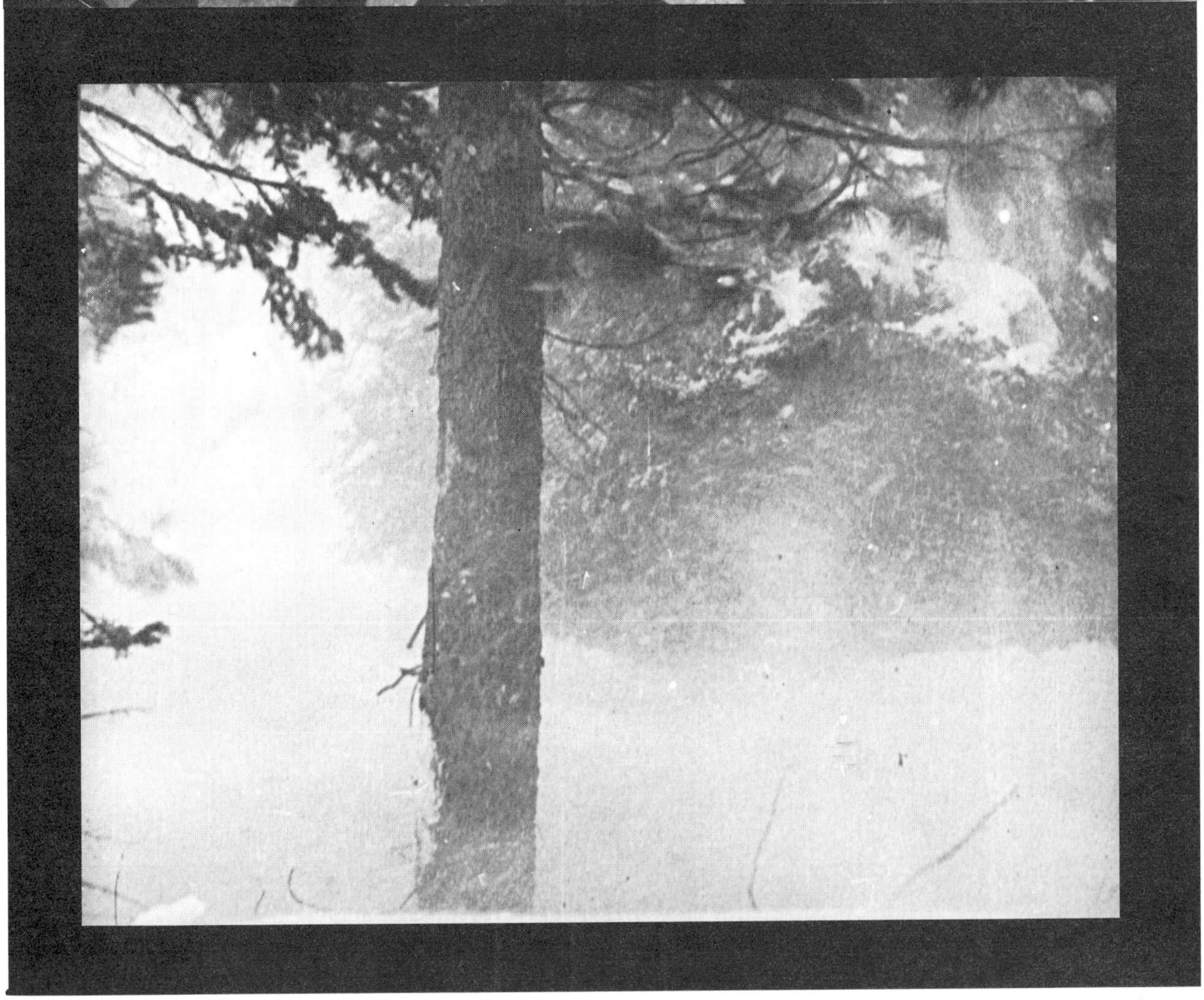

Fields:
Who's there?

Constable:
Officer Postlewhistle
of the Canadian
Mounties.

Fields:
Hello, officer.

Constable:
Good evening,
Mr. Snavely.

Fields:
Is it still snowing?

Constable:
I don't know.
To tell you the truth,
I never looked.

Fields:
Did you get
your man?

Constable:
Well, not
yet, but I got
my woman.

Fields:
Well, that's
something.

Constable: You're
pulling out?

Fields:
Figuring on going
over the
Rim tonight.

Constable: How's
your son Chester?
Did you hear from
him lately?

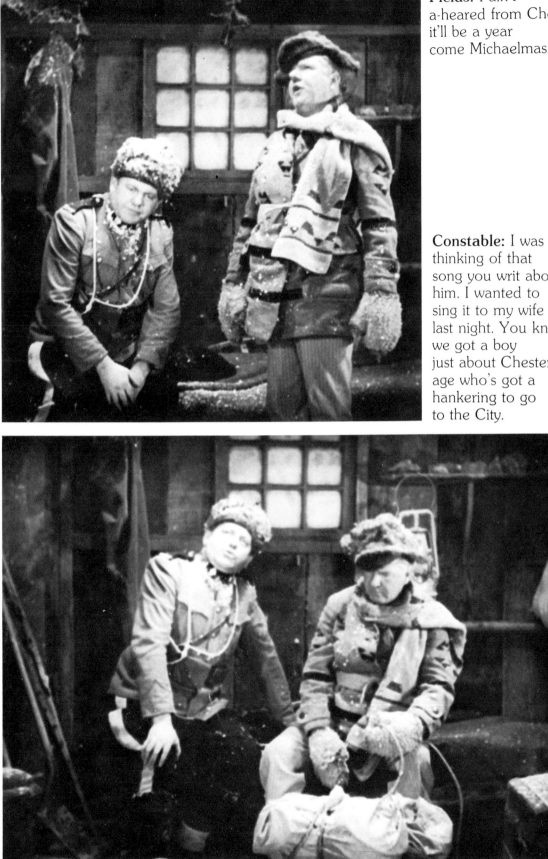

Fields: I ain't a-heared from Chester, it'll be a year come Michaelmas.

Constable: I was thinking of that song you writ about him. I wanted to sing it to my wife last night. You know, we got a boy just about Chester's age who's got a hankering to go to the City.

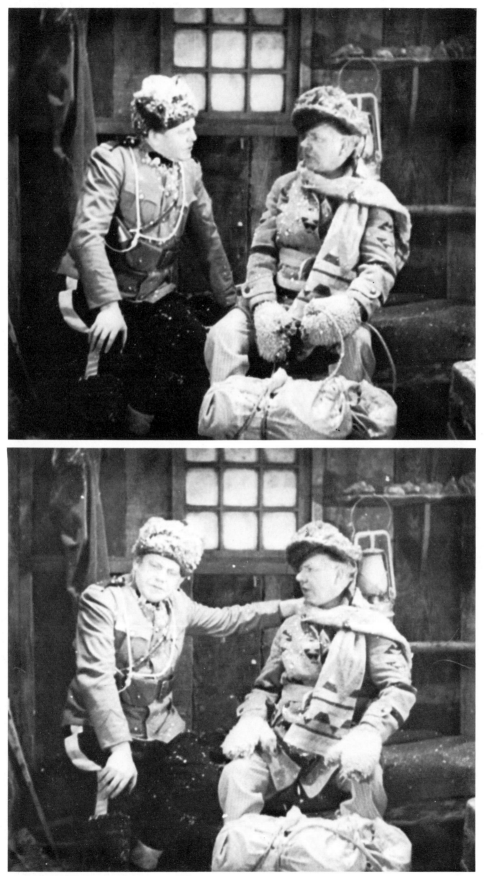

Constable: Have you got your dulcimer here?

Fields: Yes, I have, officer.

Constable: I wonder if you'd mind singing me that song.

Fields: I'd be tickled to death, sir.

Fields: You'll have to excuse me, though, if my voice isn't just right.

Fields: You
know, we can't get any
ipecac up in this
part of the country.

Constable: Go right ahead, Mr. Snavely.

Fields: You won't consider me rude if I play with my mitts on, will you?

Constable: Not at all, Mr. Snavely, not at all.

Fields: *There was once a poor boy*
And he left his country home
And he came to the City to look for work.

He promised his Ma and Pa

He would lead a civilized life

And always shun that fatal first drink.

Once in the City
  He got a situation
in a brewery

And there he made the acquaintance of some college students.
  Little thought he they were demons.

For they wore
the best of clothes,

But the clothes they
        do not always make the gentleman.

And they
   tempted him
to drink

And they
   said he
was a coward

Until at last he took the fatal glass of beer.

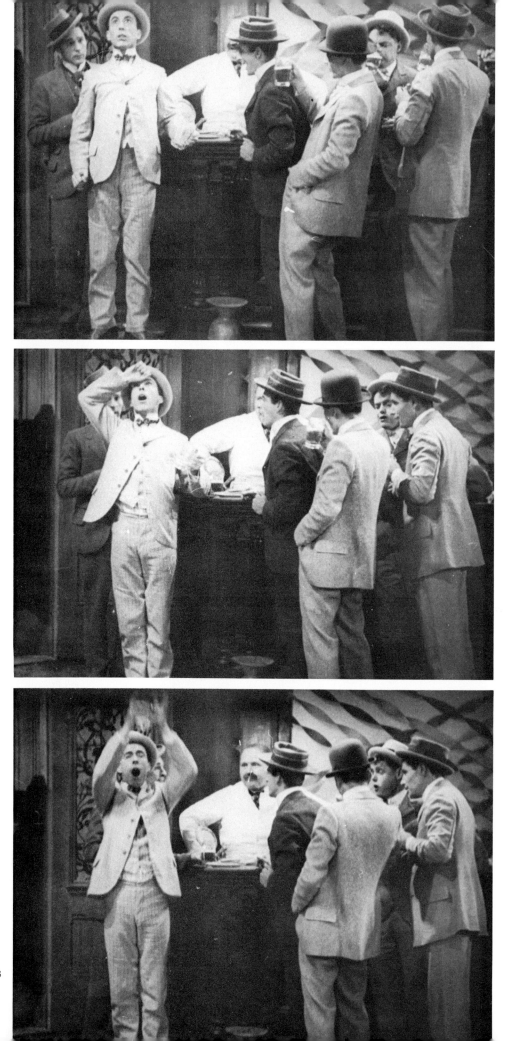

When he
found what
he'd done

He dashed
the glass
upon the floor

And he
staggered
through the door
with delirium
tremens.

Once upon the sidewalk

He met a Salvation Army girl

And wickedly he broke her tambourine.

And she said: "Well, heaven bless you!"

And placed a mark upon his brow

With a kick she
learned before she
had been saved.

There's a moral to young men

Who come down to the city...

Don't go around breaking people's tambourines.

Constable: It certainly is a sad song.

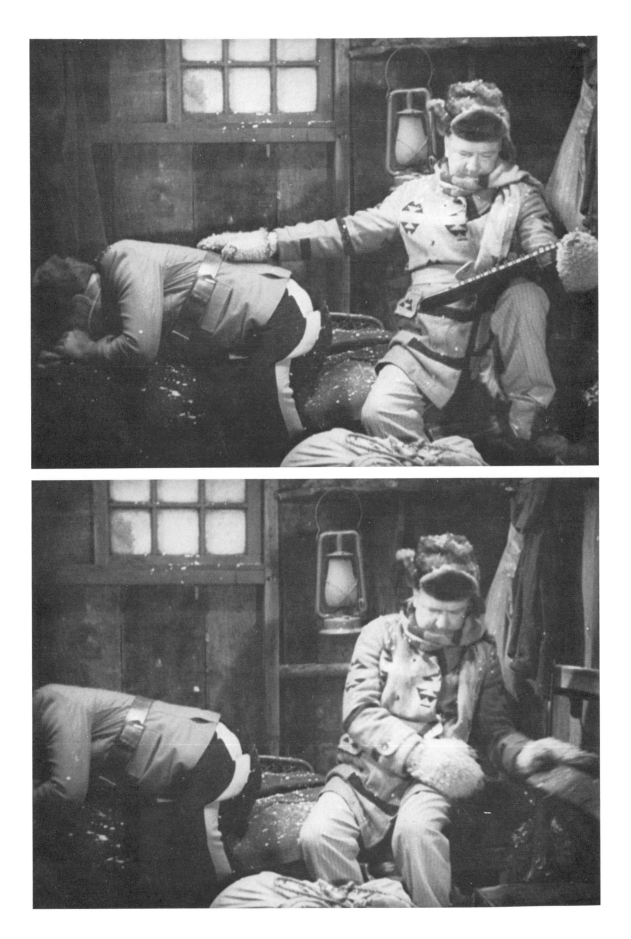

Fields: Don't cry, constable. It is a sad song. My uncle Ichabod said: "Speaking of the city, it ain't no place for women, gal, but pretty men go there."

Fields: He always said something to make you split your sides laughing. Honorable old gentleman he was.

Fields: Well, I think I'll be hightailing it over the Rim.

Fields:
And it ain't a
fit night out for
man or beast.

39

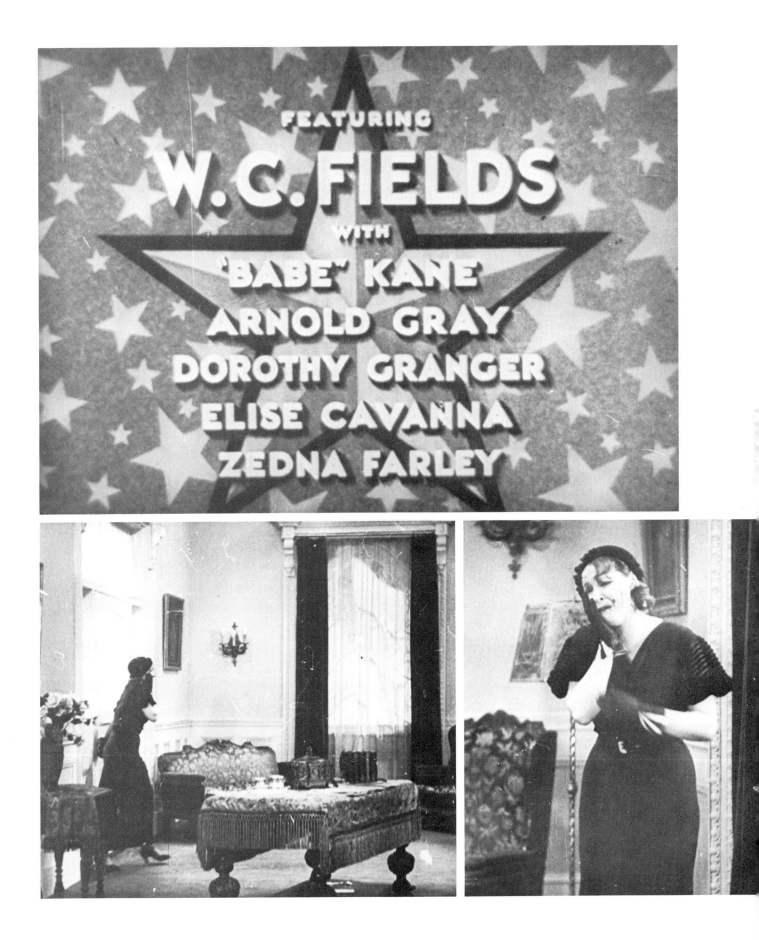

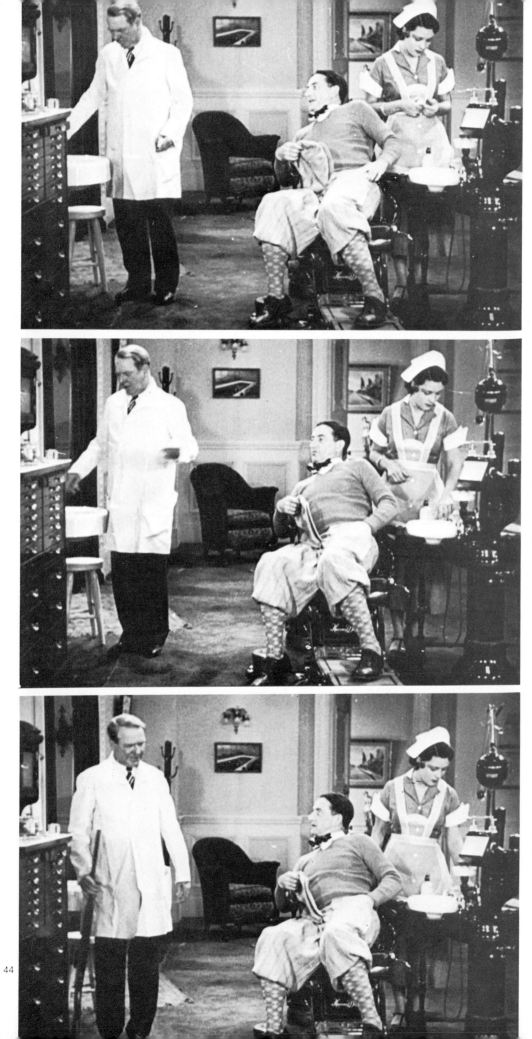

Man: How about
tomorrow, doc?
Fields:
What time?
Man: Oh, about . . .

Fields:
No, I won't be
able to go.
Man: Why not?

Fields: I'm
going duck
shooting.

Man: Well, I'm going home.

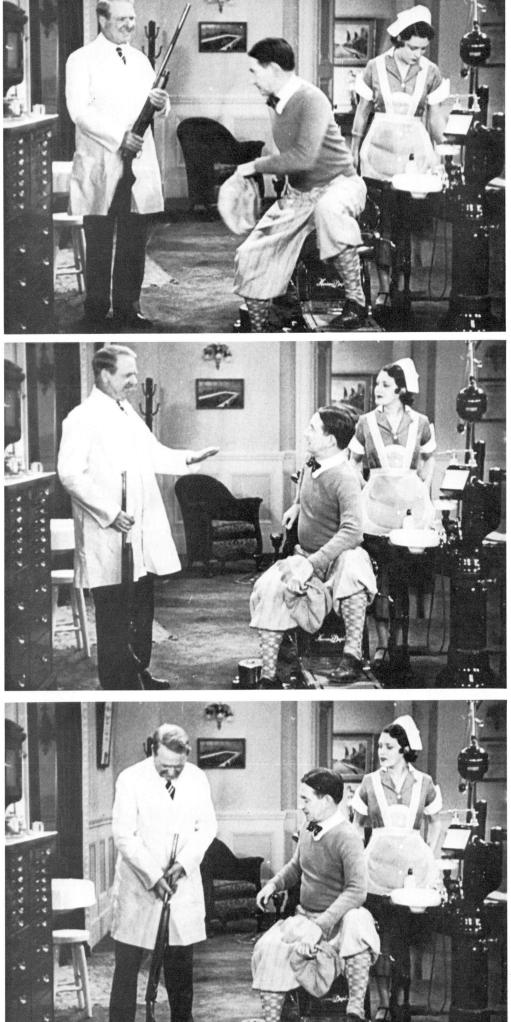

Fields: You should have been there.

Fields: I took this mashie niblick,

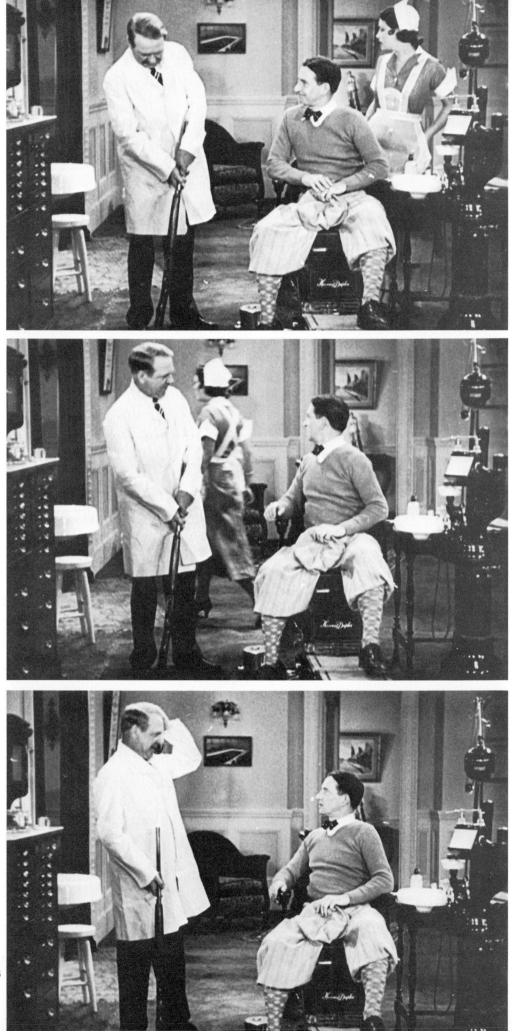

Fields: and
hit a straight shot
for the pin.

Fields:
It beaned
the old geezer.

Fields:
Down into the
water connection
it goes . . .

Fields: Oh,
the hell with her.

47

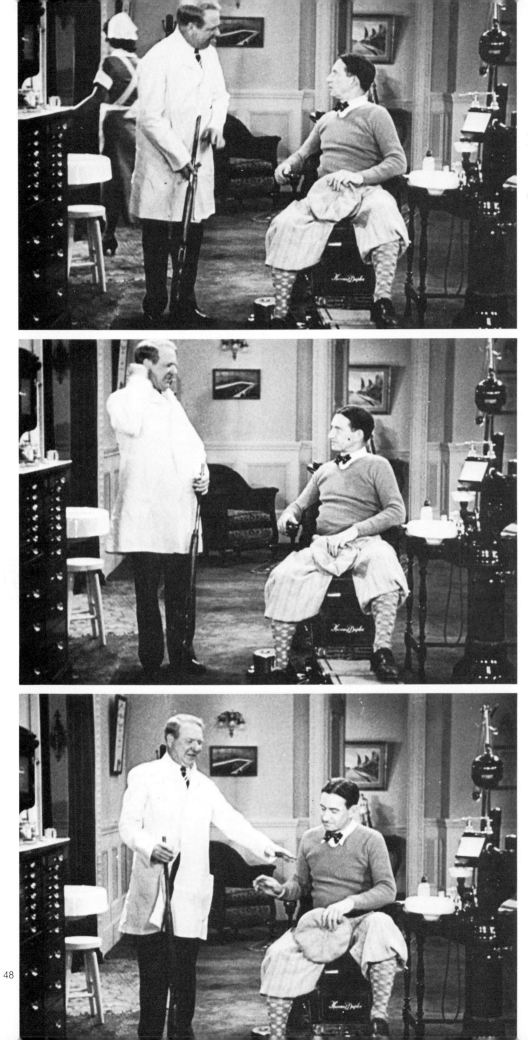

Fields:
. . . dropped into the water connection,

Fields:
I picked it up and dropped it over my shoulder,

Fields:
and down into the hole it goes.

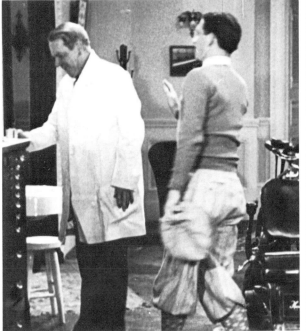

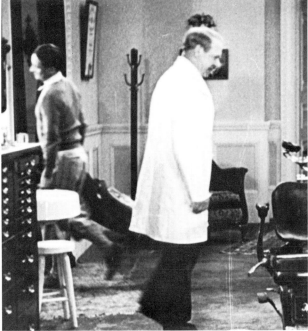

Man: Well, I'll give you a ring tomorrow, doc.
Fields: OK. Boy, was he burned up.

Fields: You could have fried eggs on the back of his neck.

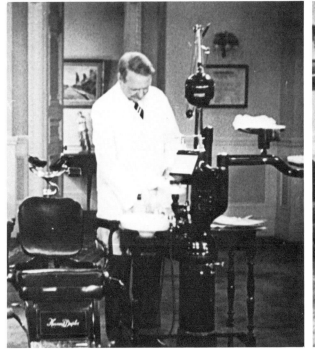

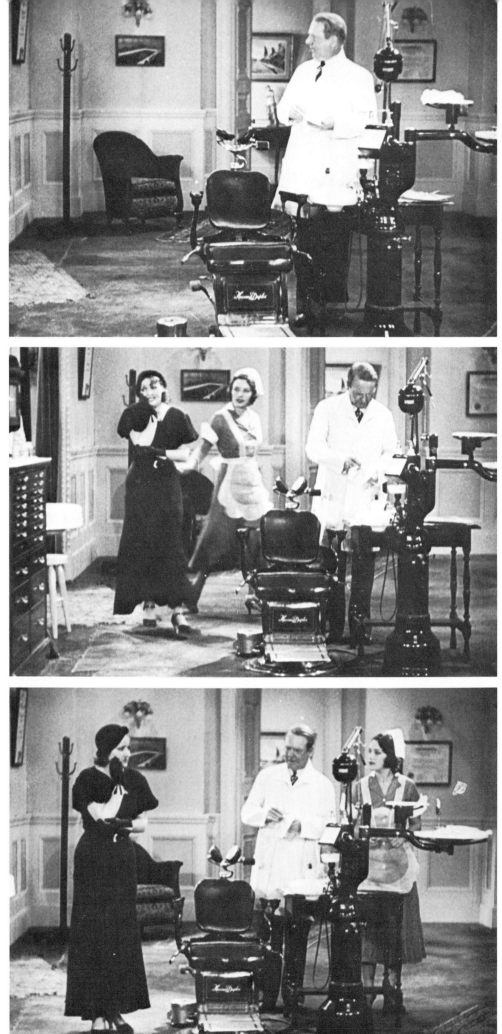

Fields:
Send her in.

Fields:
How're you doing?
You want to sit
down?

Fields:
Put it in
here, please.

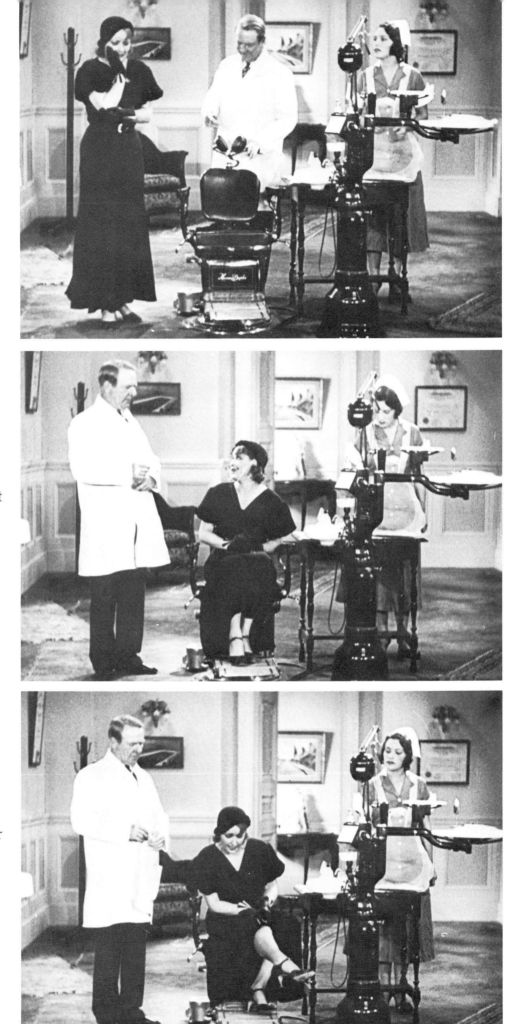

Patient: You won't
hurt my legs,
will you?

Patient: My doctor
says I have a
very bad leg.

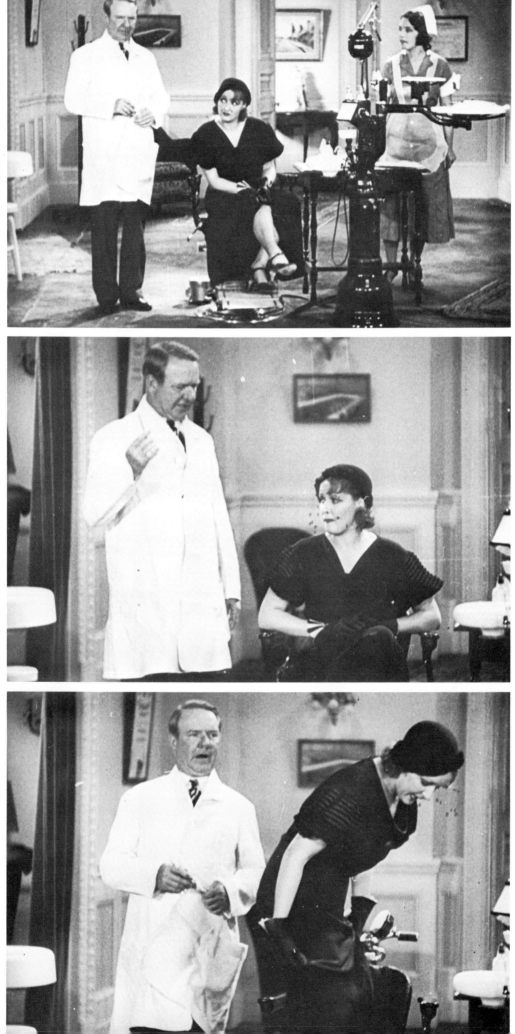

Fields:
Your doctor is off his nut. I don't believe in doctors anyway.

Fields:
There's a doctor lives right down the street here. He treated a man for yellow jaundice for nine years; then he found out he was a Jap.

Patient: You know, a little dog bit me.

52

Patient: Bit me right here.

Fields: Dog bit you?

Patient: Yes. It was a little dachshund, little tiny dog. Right behind me, and bit me right there.

Patient: I'm standing with my back turned and there he was, this little dog, and he bit me right here.

53

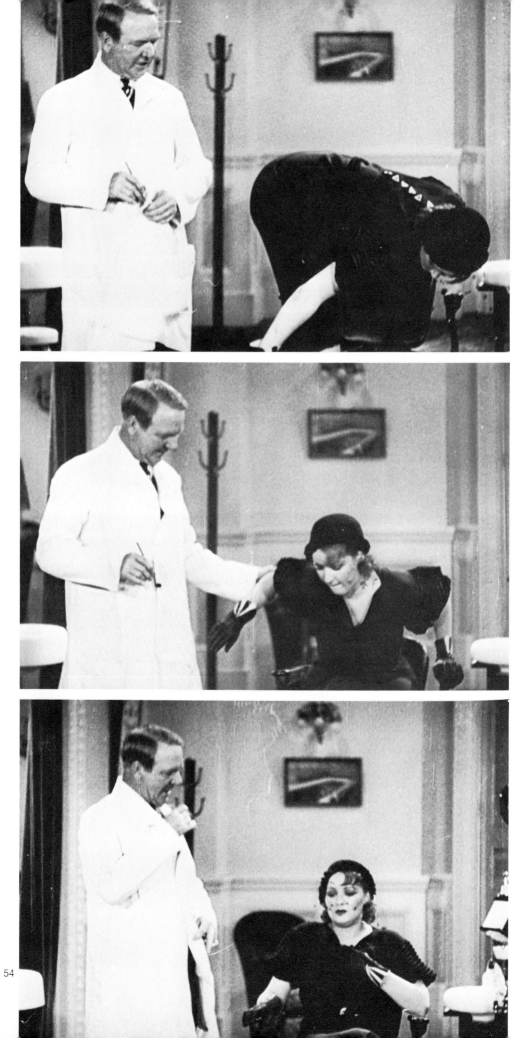

Fields: You're rather fortunate it wasn't a Newfoundland dog that bit you.

Fields: Will you sit down.

Fields: You want gas?

Patient: Oh, gas or
electric lights.
I'd feel nervous
to have you
fool around
me in the
dark.

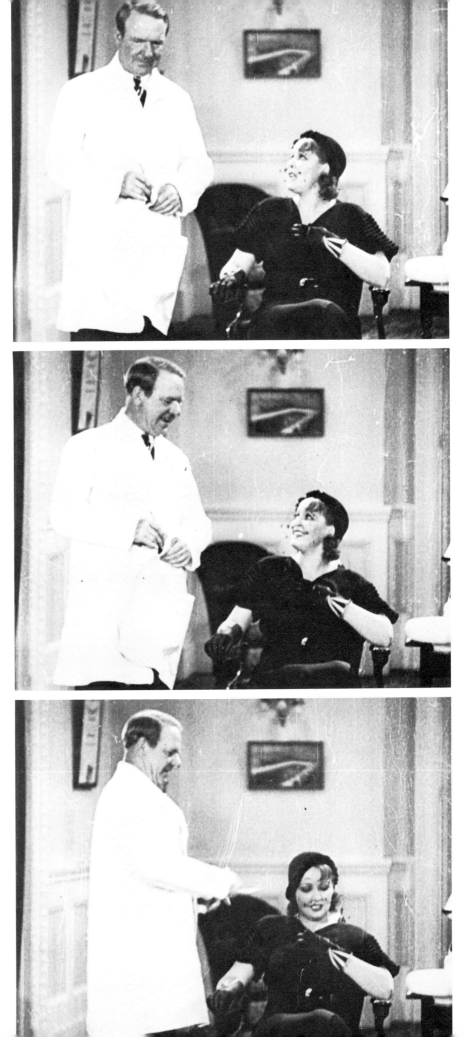

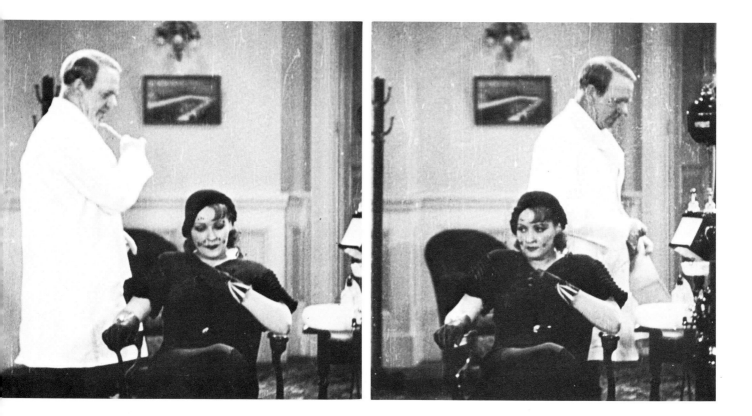

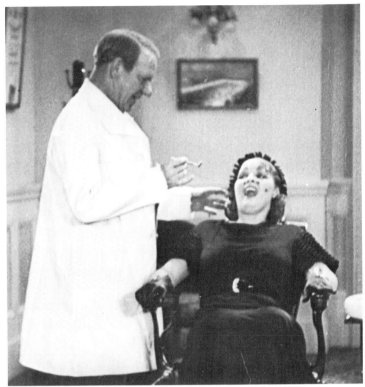

Fields: Come on,

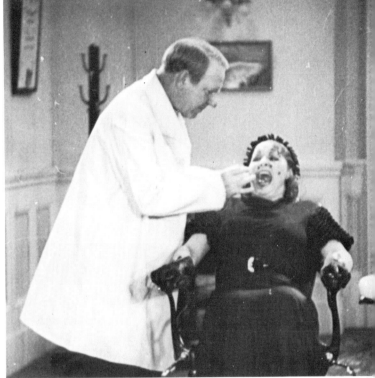

Fields: come on, now.

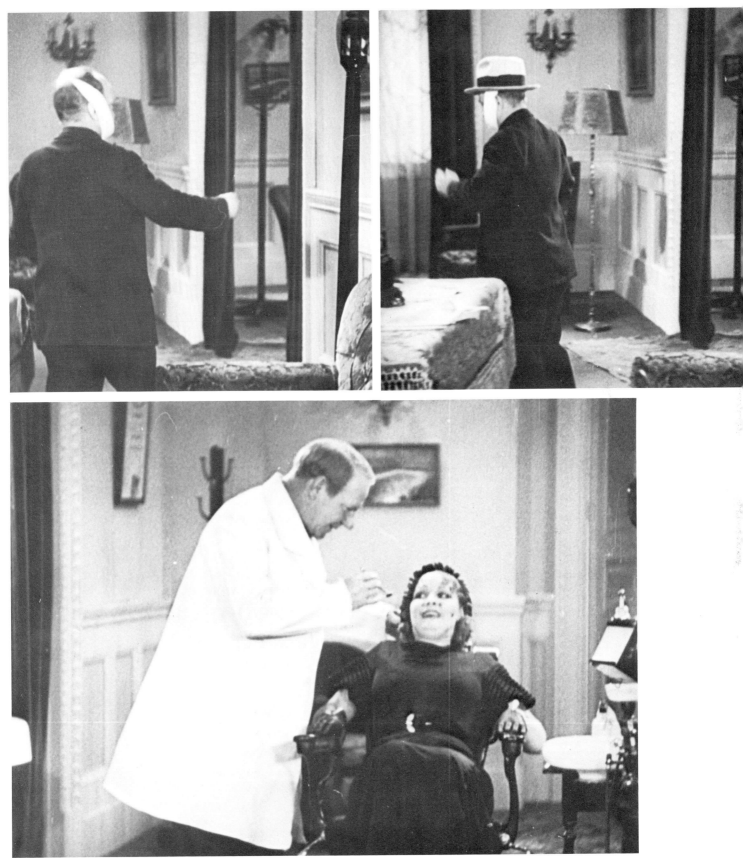

Fields: I'll try not to be so cruel this time.

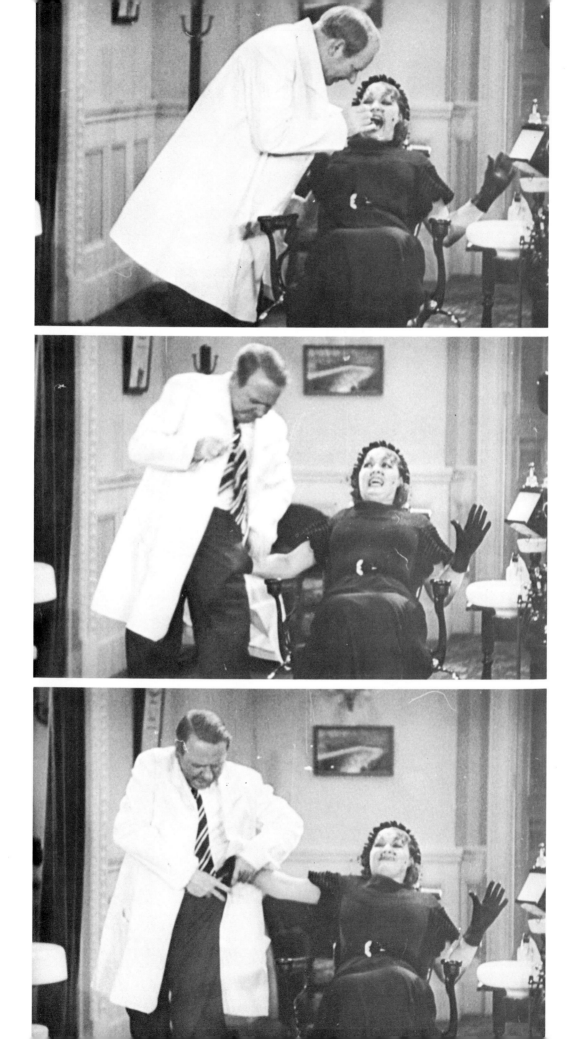

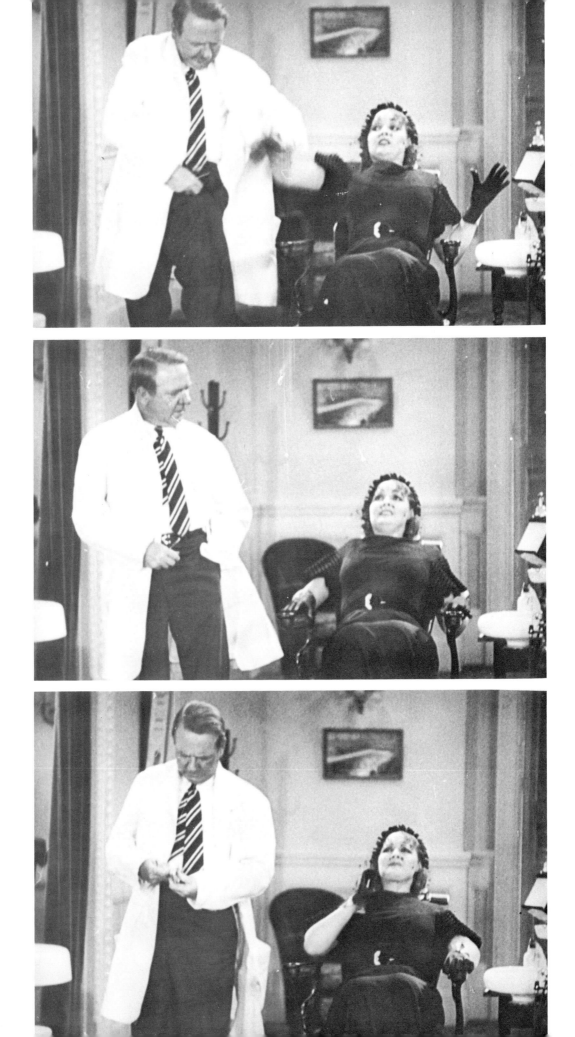

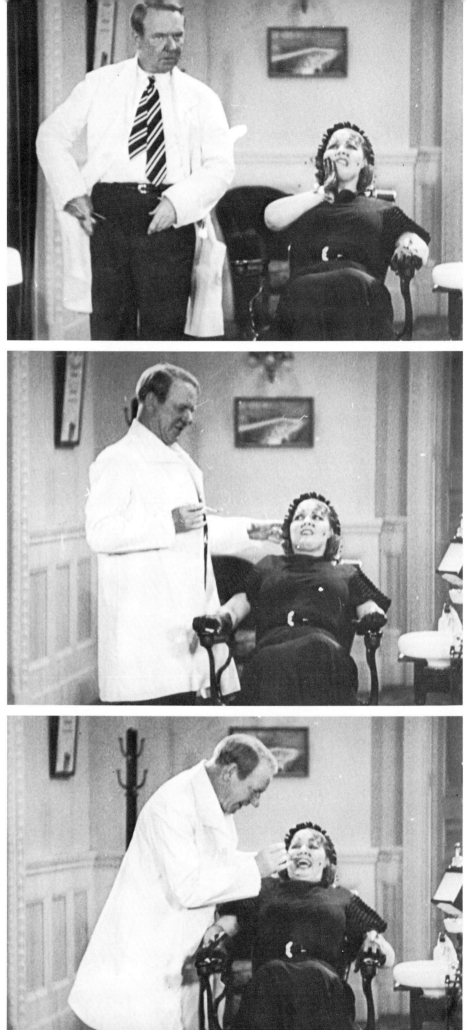

Fields: Come on, come on.

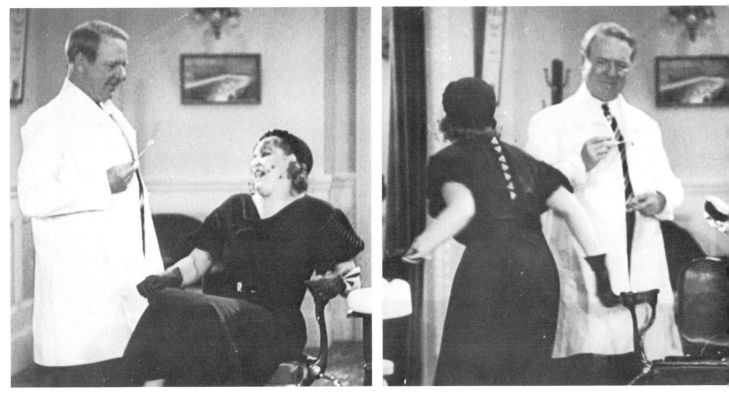

Patient: Oh, doctor, I can't let you do that again!

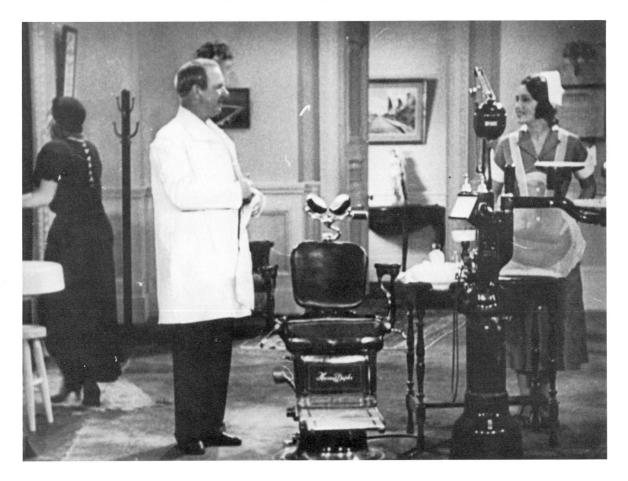

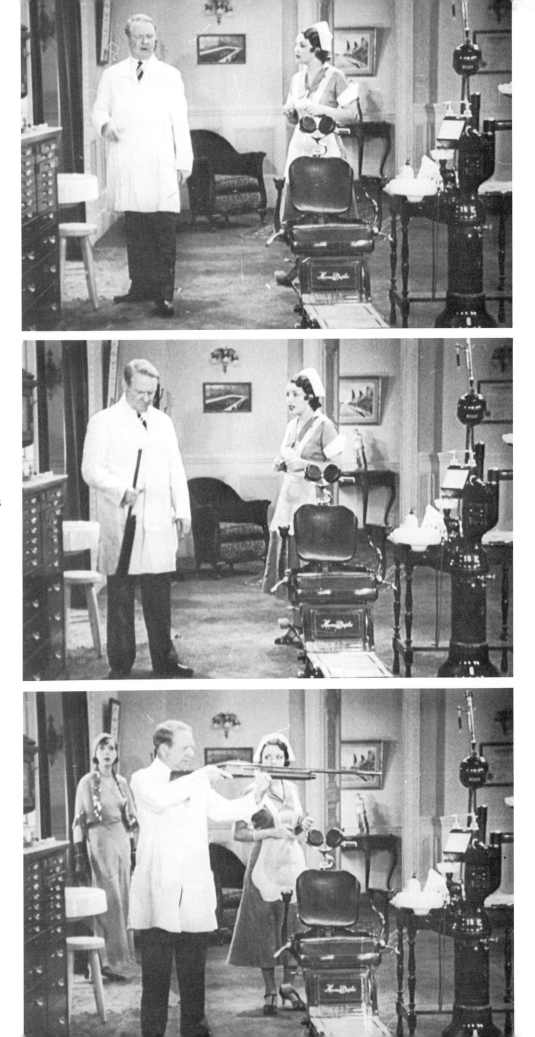

Fields:
Tell her
I'm out.

Nurse: But,
doctor, she has
a three-o'clock
appointment.

Fields:
Well, tell
her she has
a four-o'clock
appointment.

Fields:
Why, when
I was in
Darjeeling...

Fields:
Tell her I'm out.

Fields:
Go out there
and tell her
I'm out.

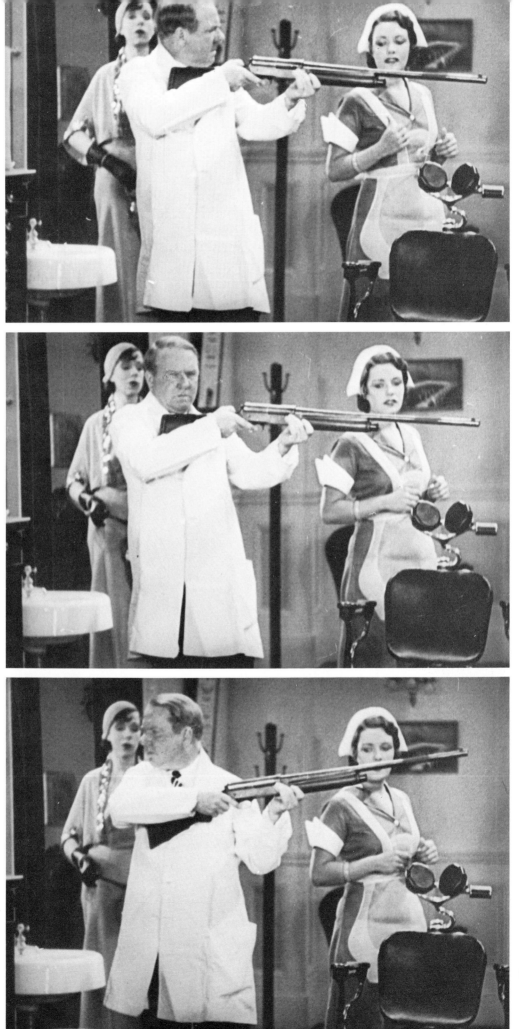

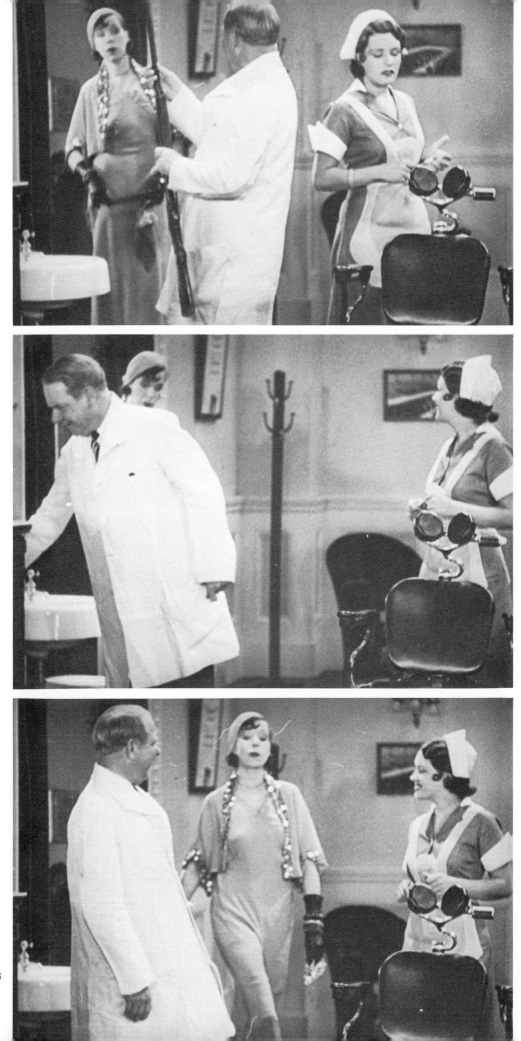

Fields:
How do you
do, how do
you do.

Fields:
We've been
waiting for
you. Sit down.

Fields:
When I tell
you to go
out there and
tell one of
these palookas
that I'm out,

Fields:
. . . go out there
and tell them
I'm out.

Fields:
Don't have
these buzzards
walk in
on me.

71

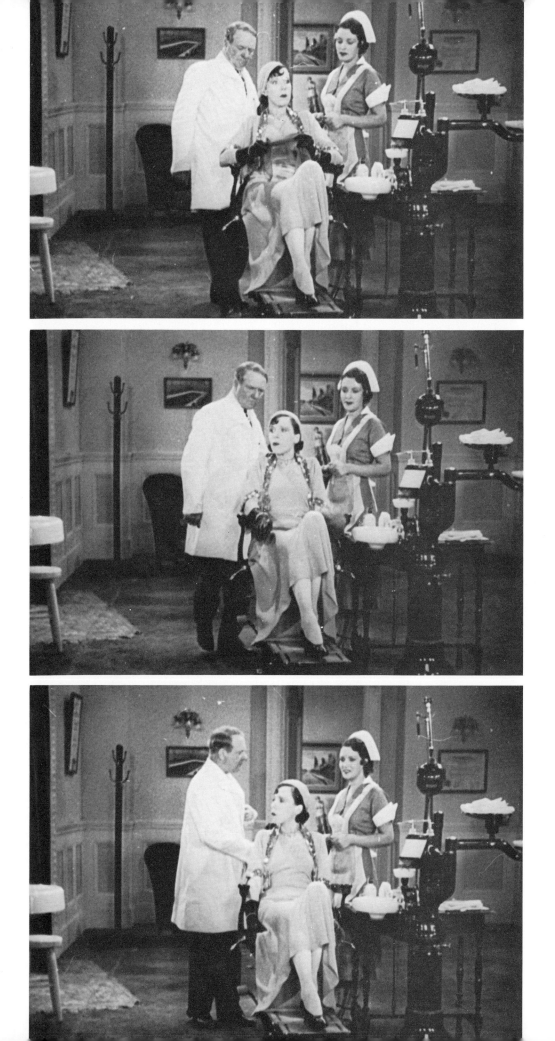

Fields: You just came in for the ride?

Fields: Haven't I seen your face somewhere before?

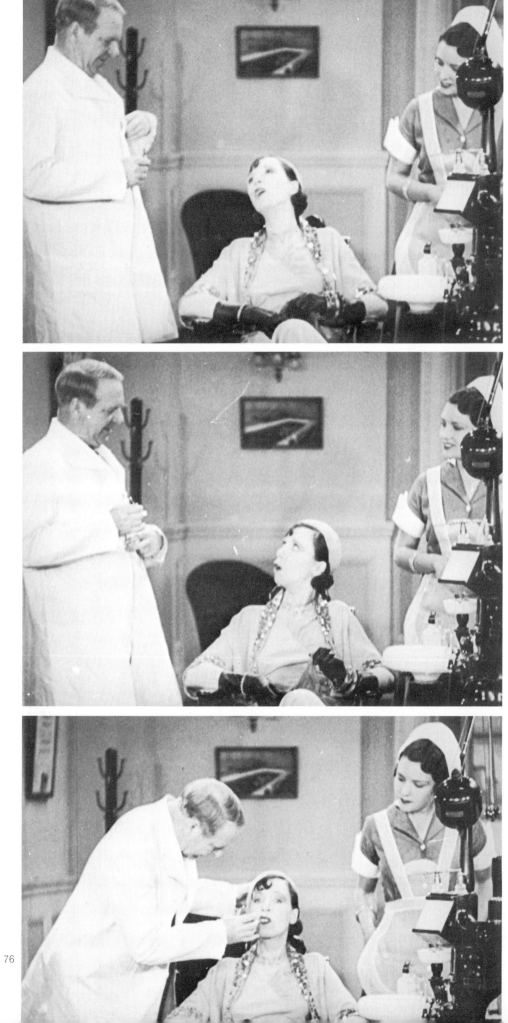

Patient: Oh, probably you've seen me at the horse show.

Fields: Jockey?
Patient: Sir!

Fields: Will you open your mouth?

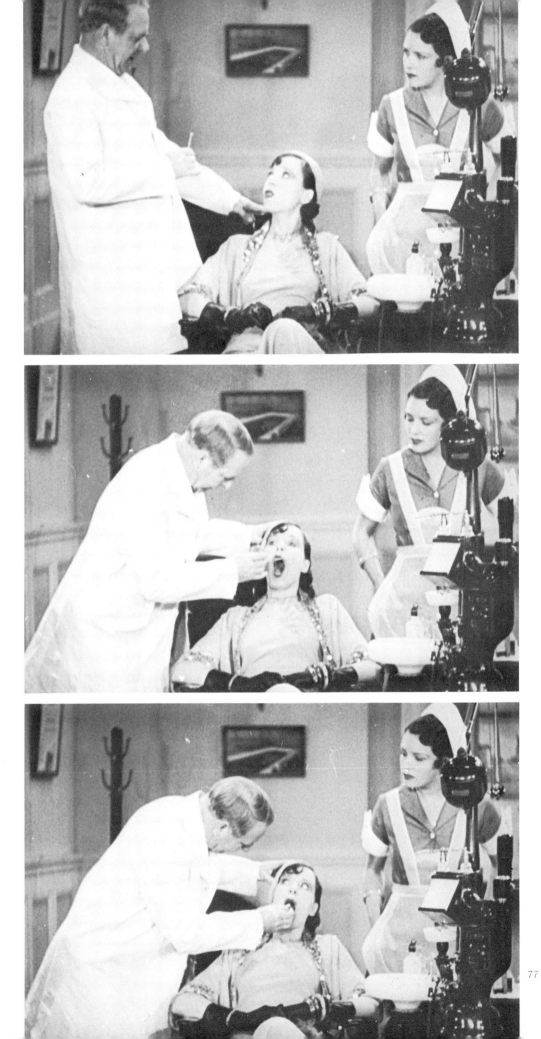

Fields:
Oh, come
on now, you've
got a bigger
mouth than that,
open it.

Fields:
Oh, beautiful . . .

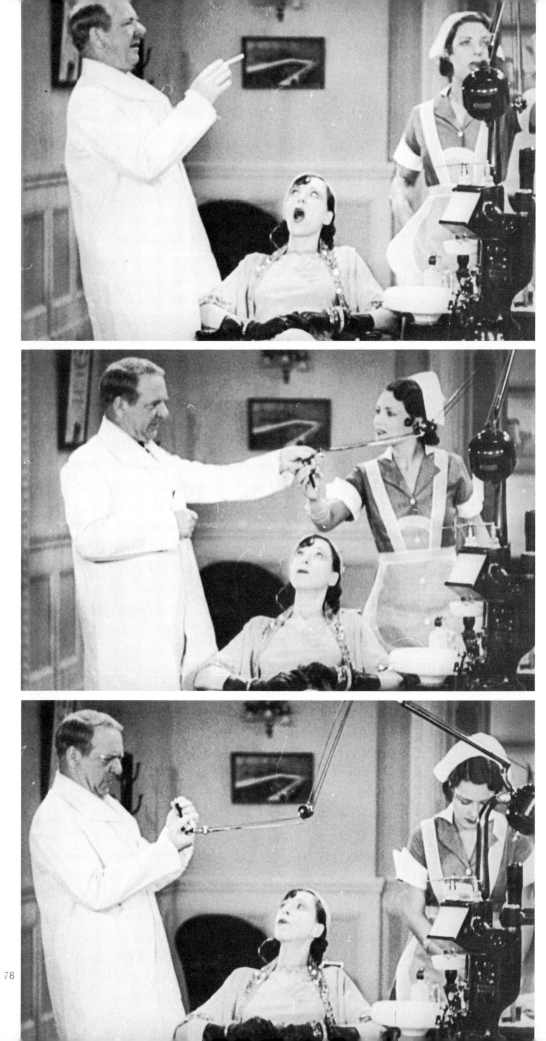

Fields:
Hand
me that
four-hundred
and-four
circular
buzz saw.

Fields:
Is that a
four-oh-four
article you
gave me?

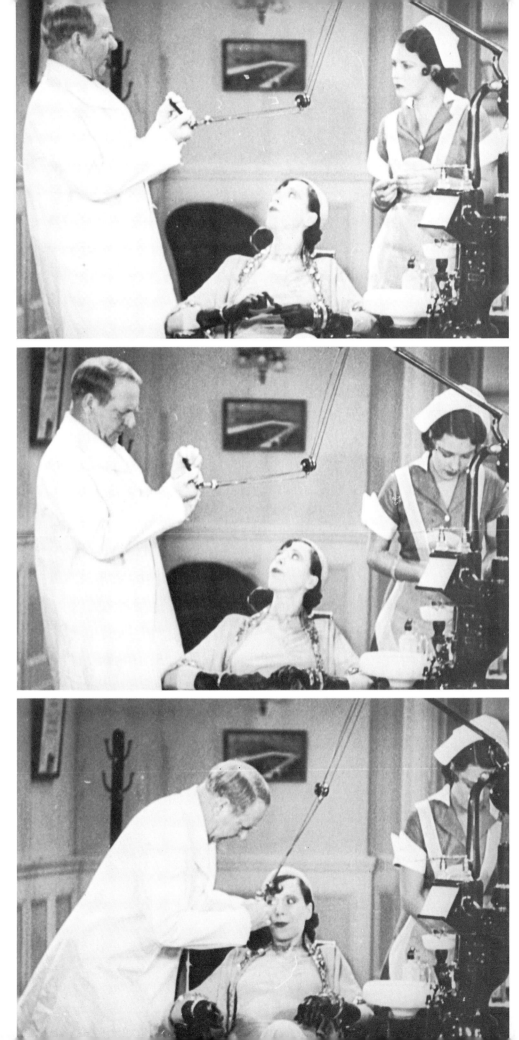

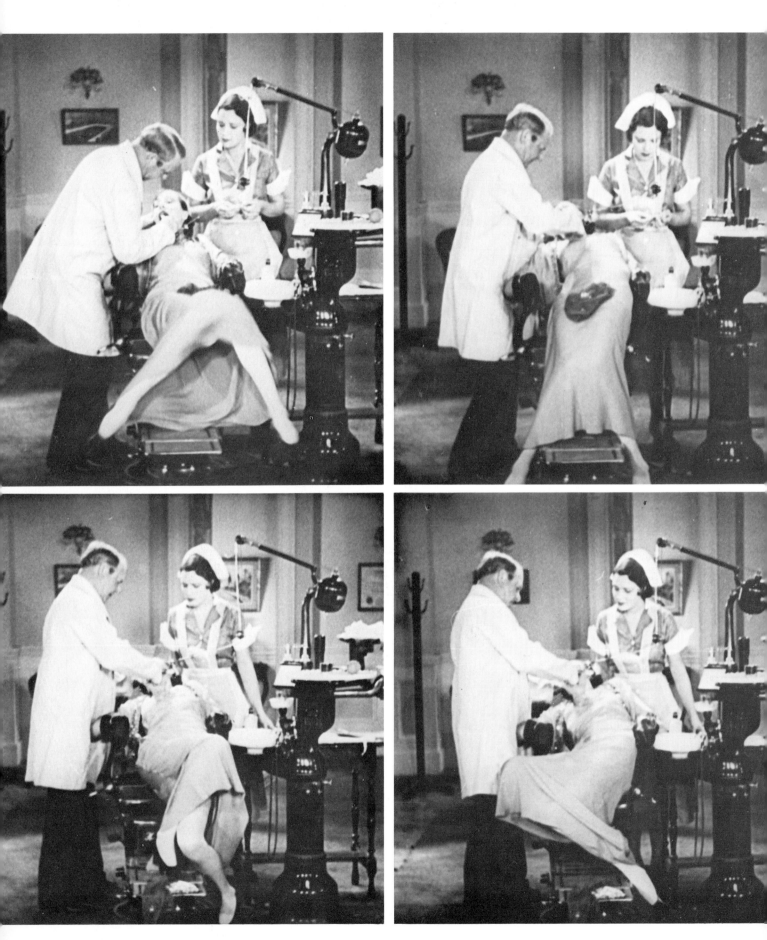

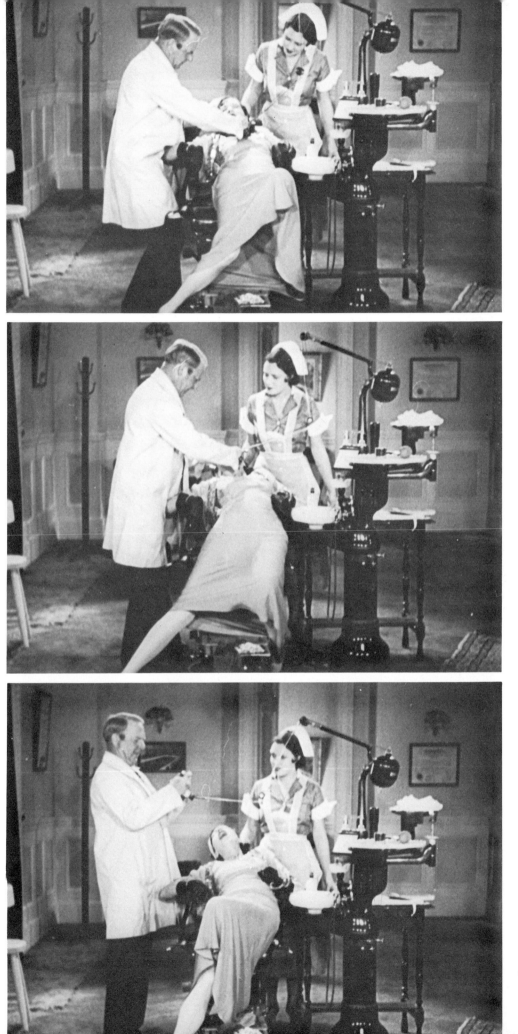

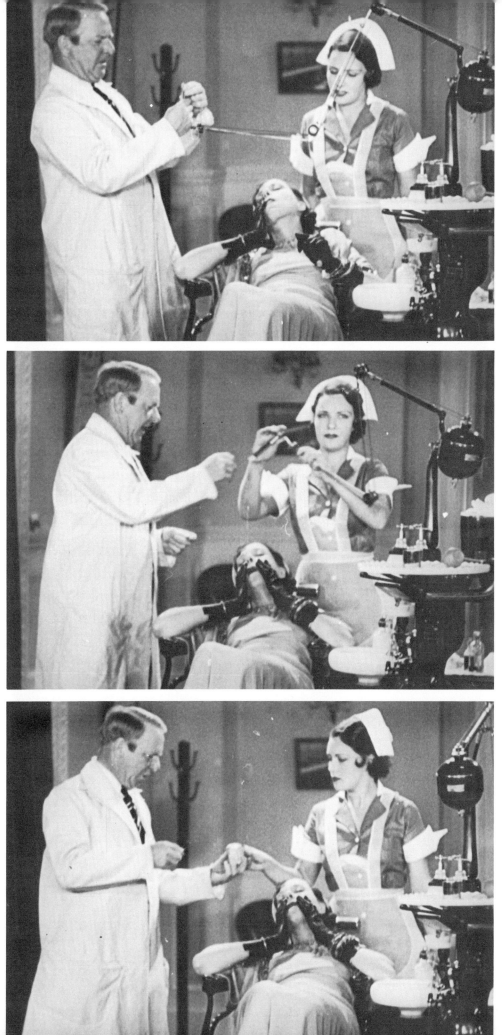

Fields: Here we are.

Fields: That didn't hurt, did it?

82

Fields:
I knew it
wouldn't
hurt you.

Fields:
Give me
that packing,
please.

Fields:
Pardon
me for just
a moment.

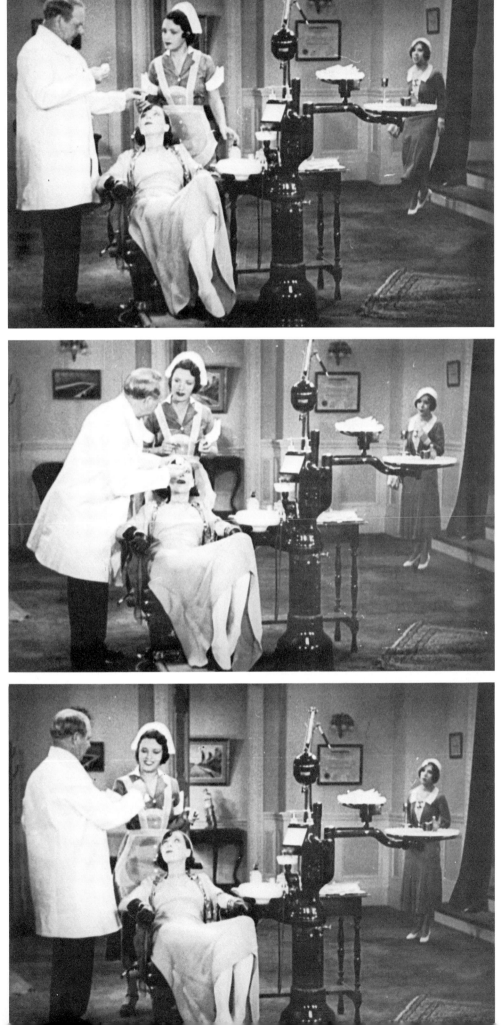

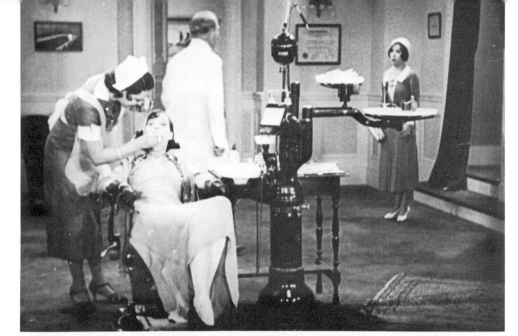

Daughter: You wouldn't let Arthur come and see me, so I'm going to see him!

Fields: Excuse me a moment, folks.

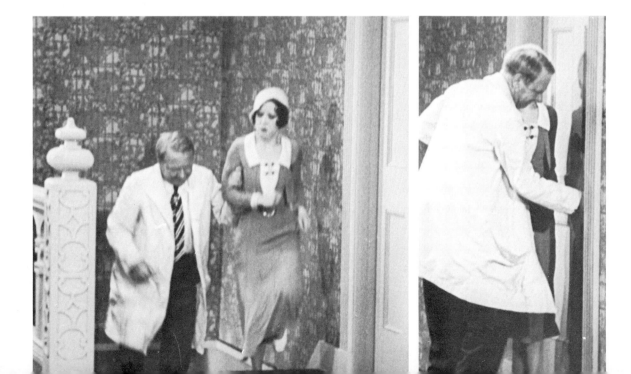

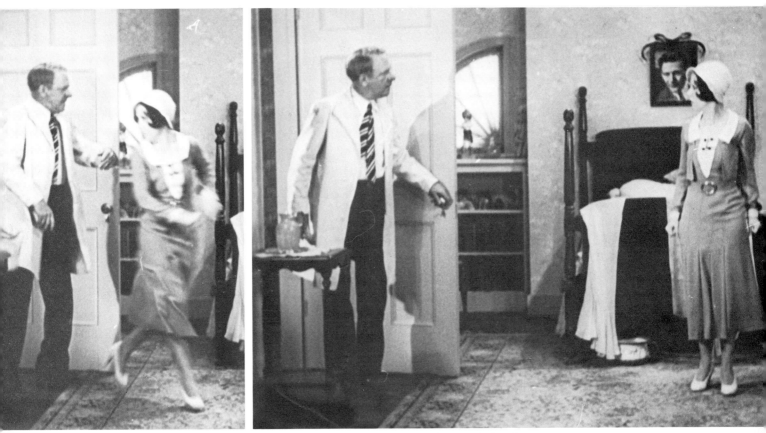

Fields: Stay in there. **Fields:** Now, what do you think of that?

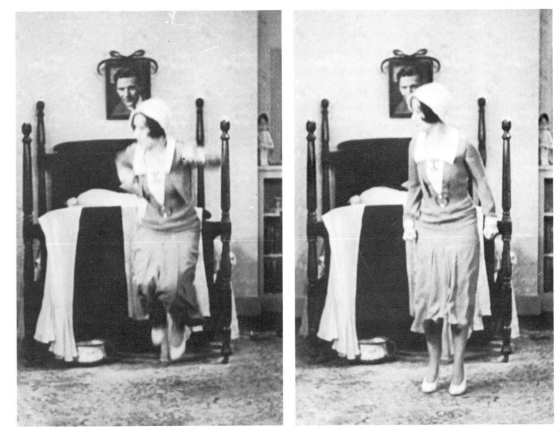

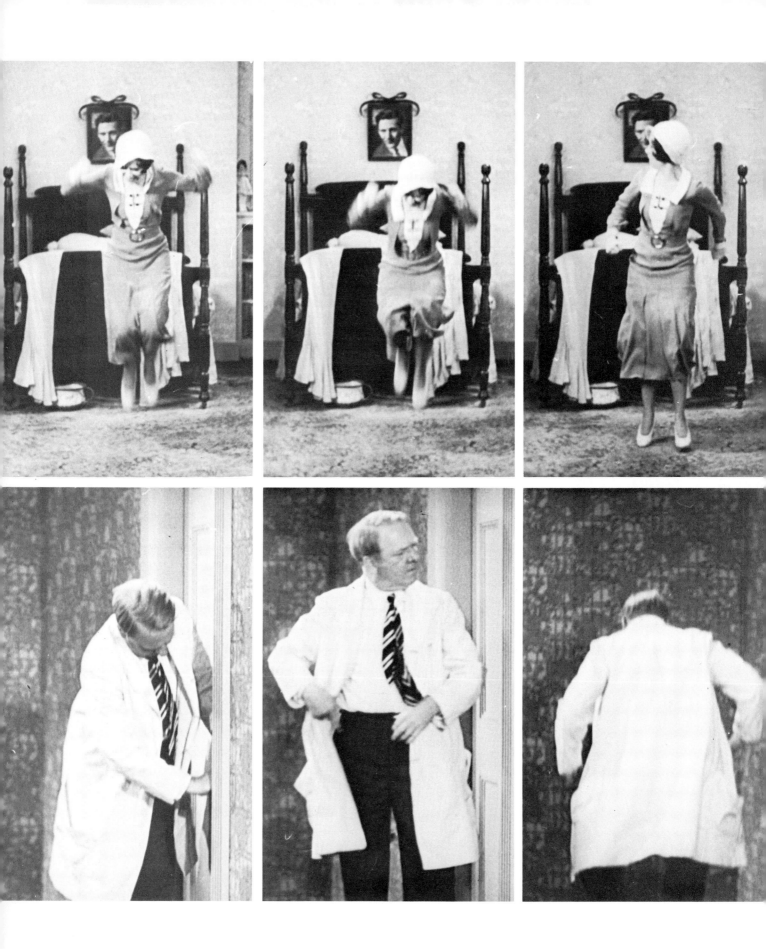

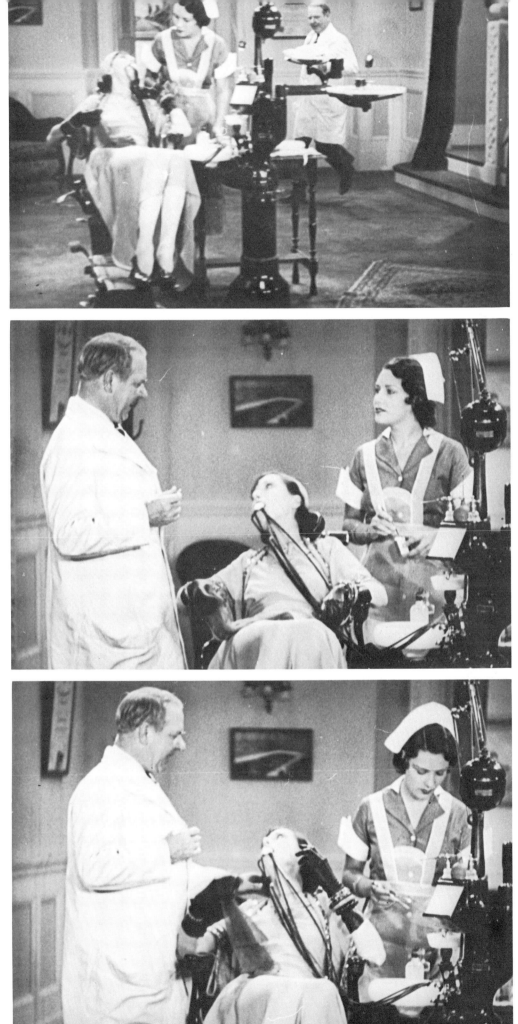

Fields: Keep
you waiting?

Fields:
You said a
mouthful there.

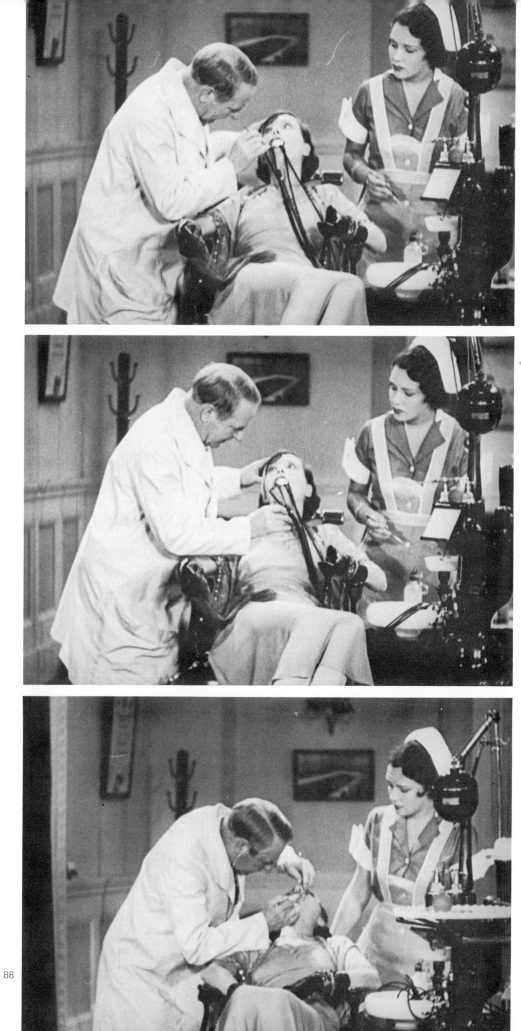

Fields: Are
all your lines
busy?

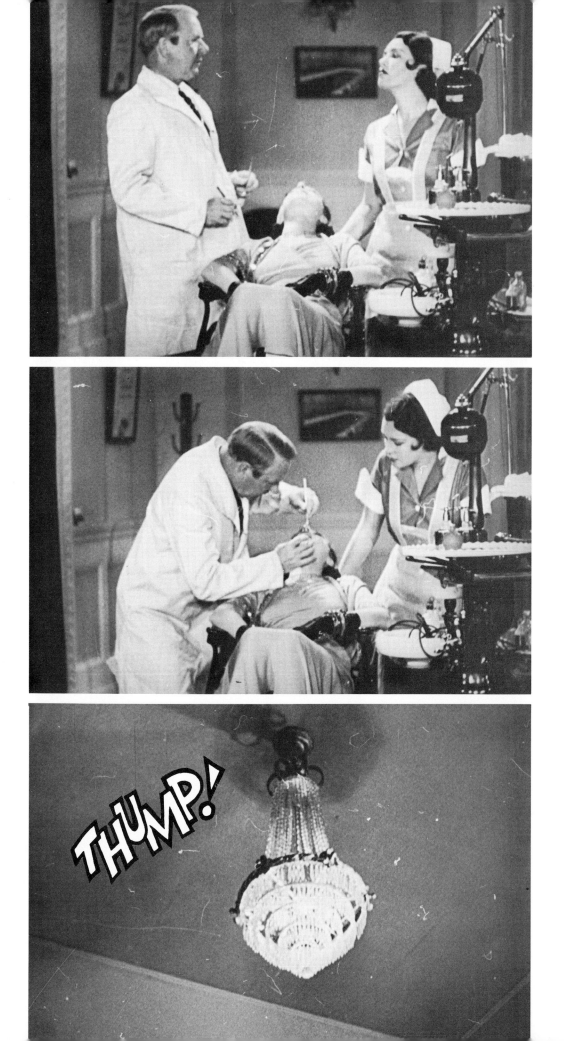

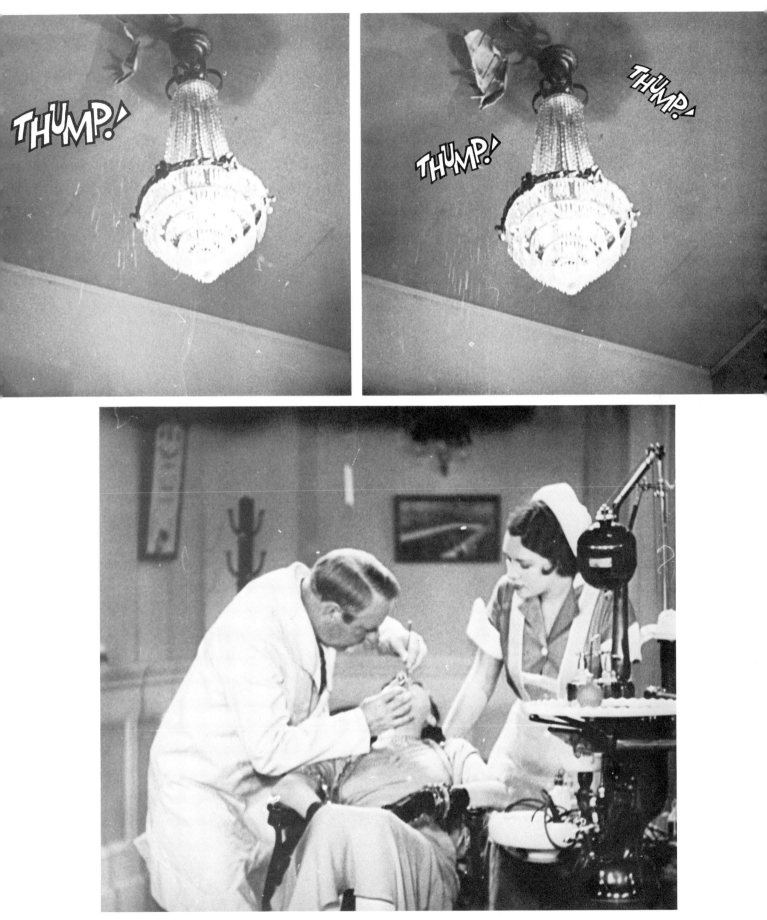

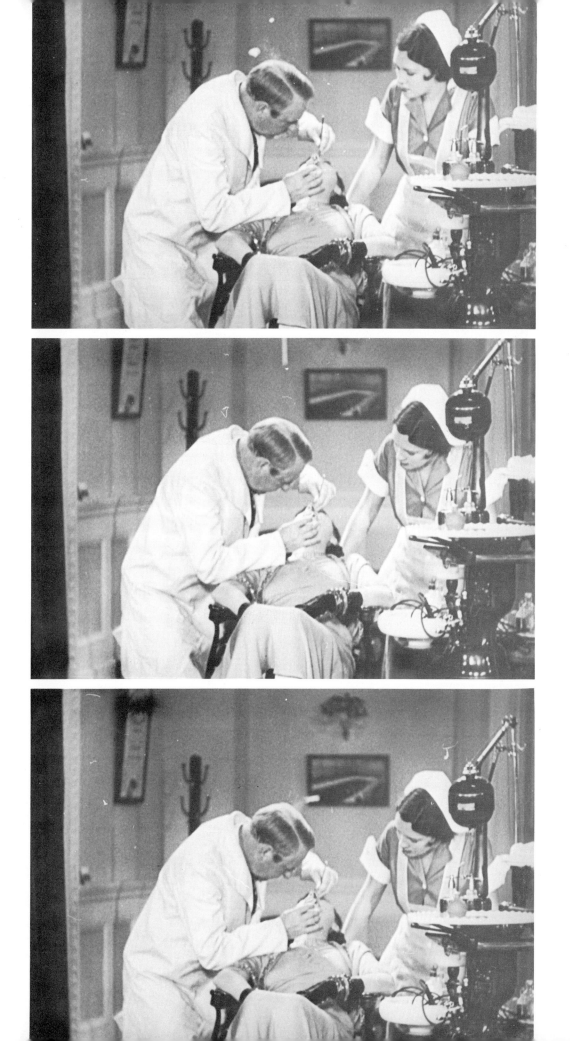

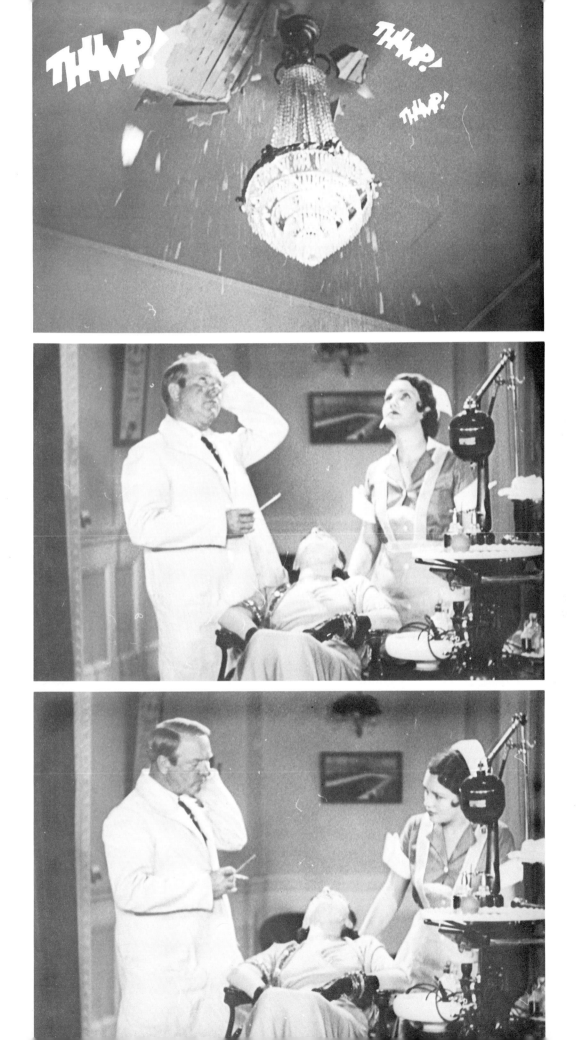

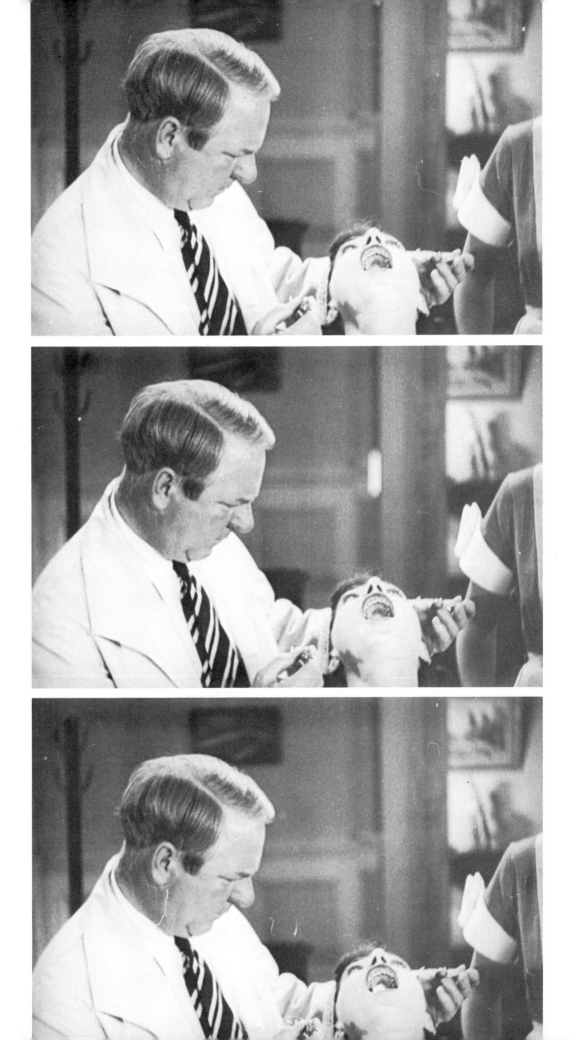

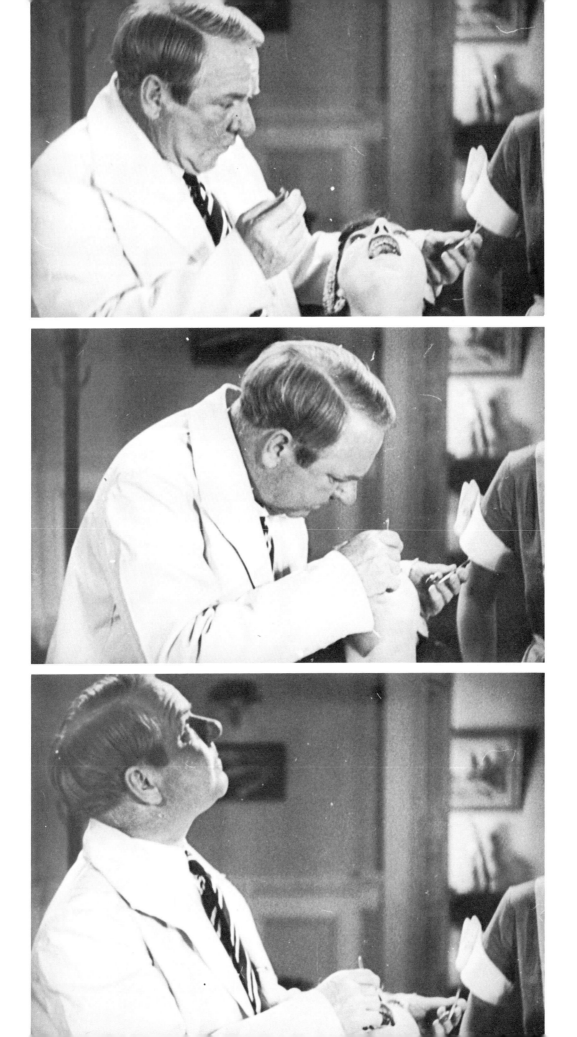

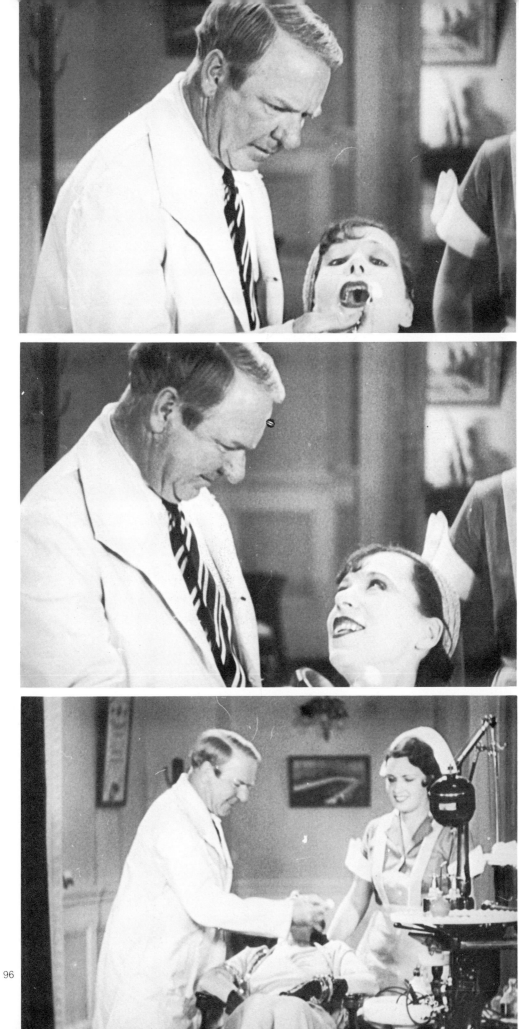

Patient: Well, it came out easily, didn't it?

Fields: Yes, it did, yes, it did.

Fields:
Excuse me
just a bit.

Fields: Open that door.
Daughter: I can't, you locked me in.

Fields: Where's the key?   **Daughter:** In your pocket.

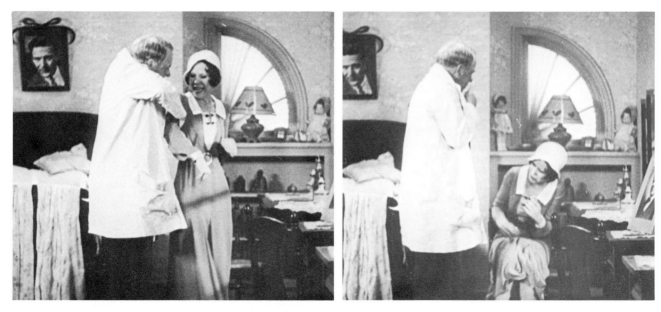

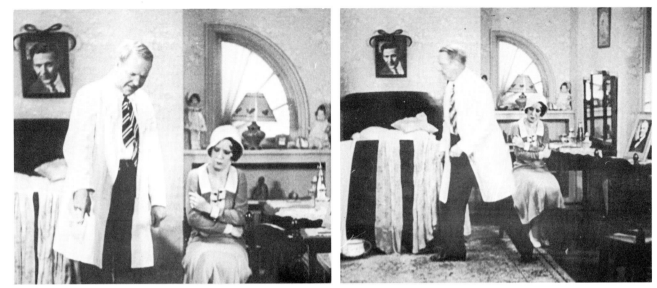

Fields: Sit there!

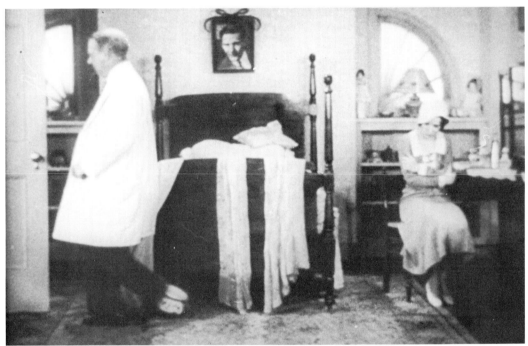

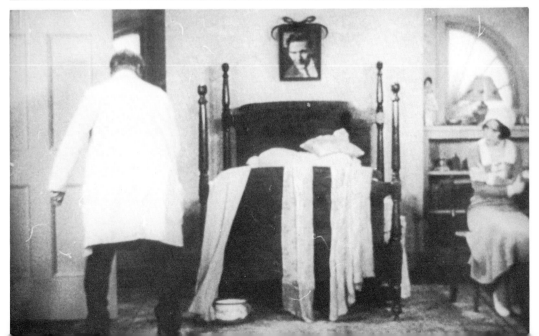

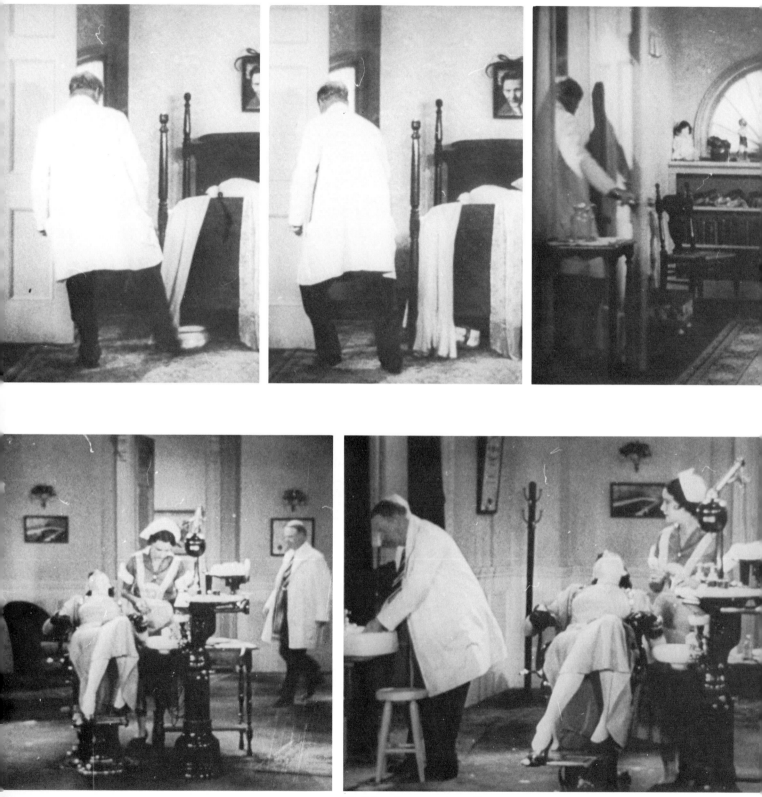

Fields: Any patients?

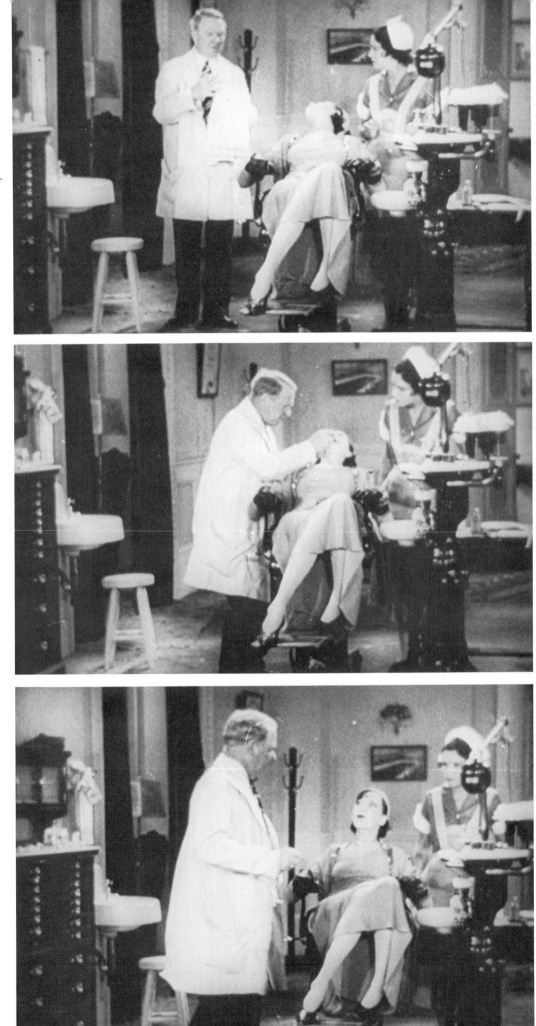

Nurse:
Miss Peyton here.

Fields:
Have you
ever had this
tooth pulled
before?
Patient: No.

Fields:
This won't
hurt you—
much.

101

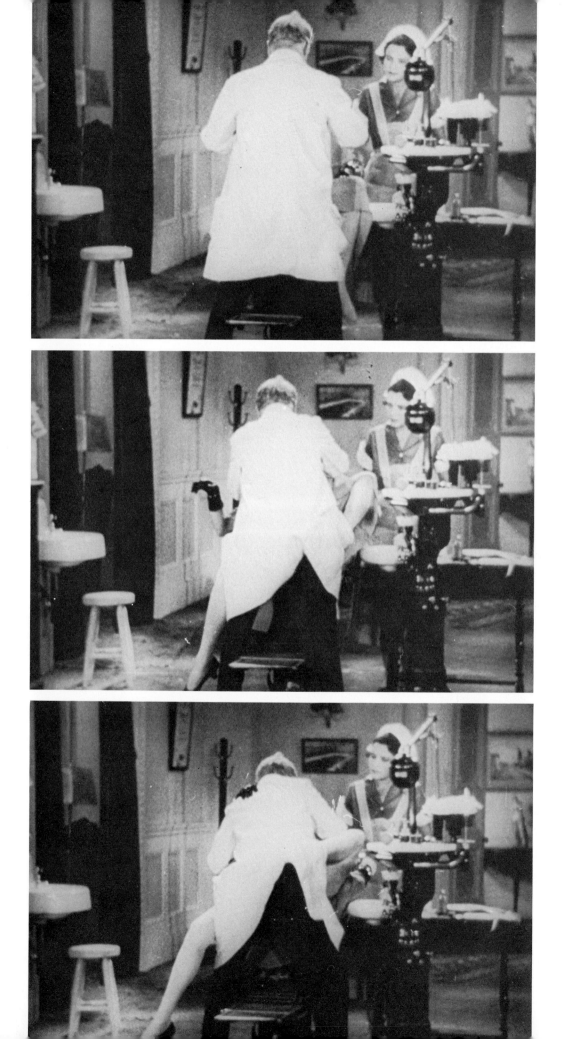

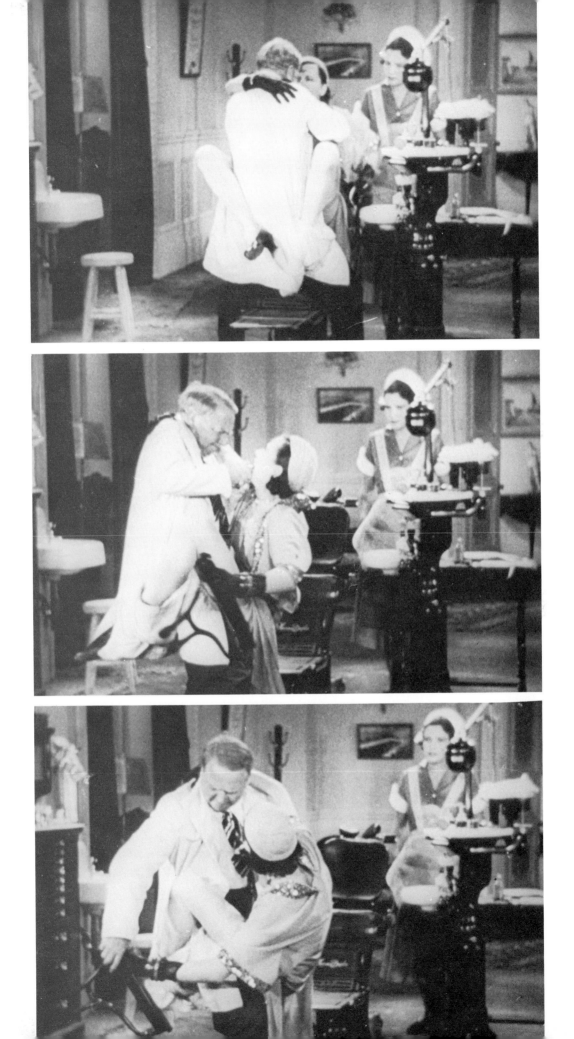

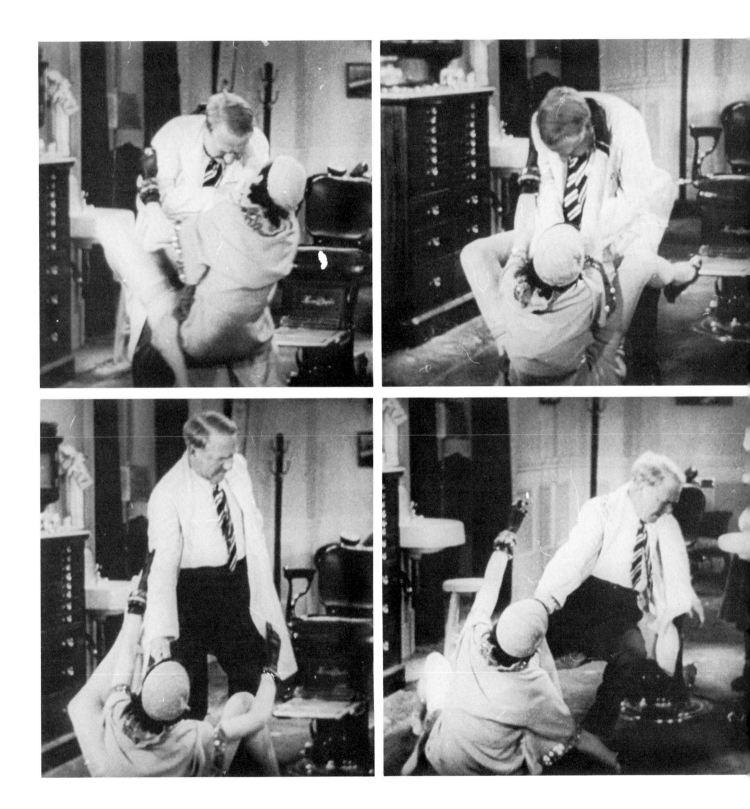

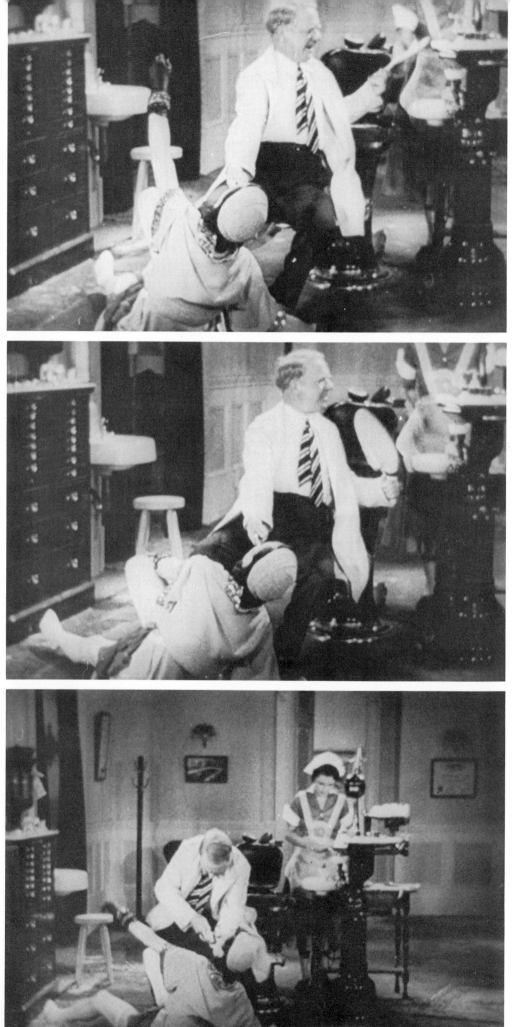

Fields:
I'm gonna give her gas.

Fields:
She's not gonna pull me around the floor.

106

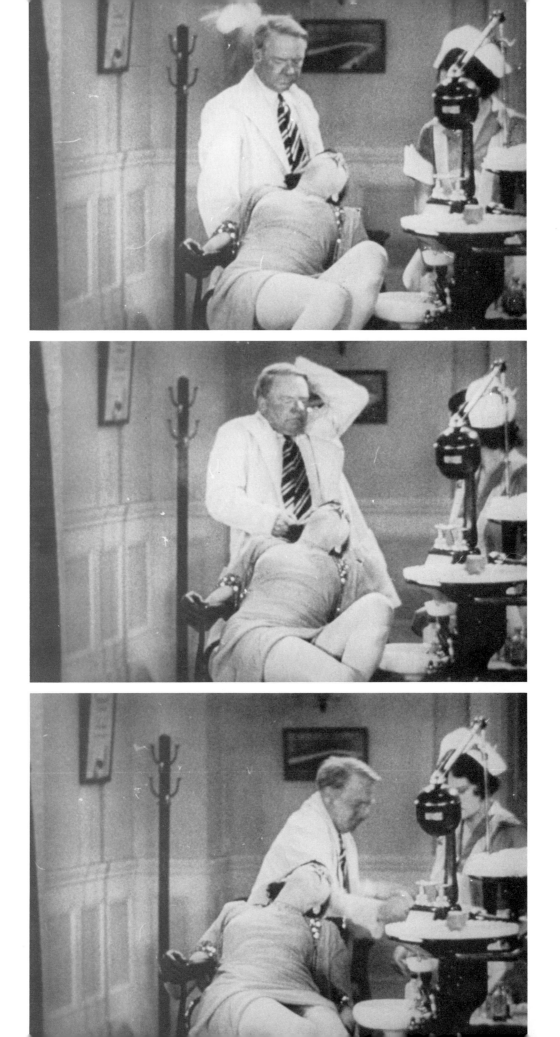

Nurse: Relax.
Would you like a drink?

Patient: What
is it?
Nurse: Water.

Patient: No, thank
you.

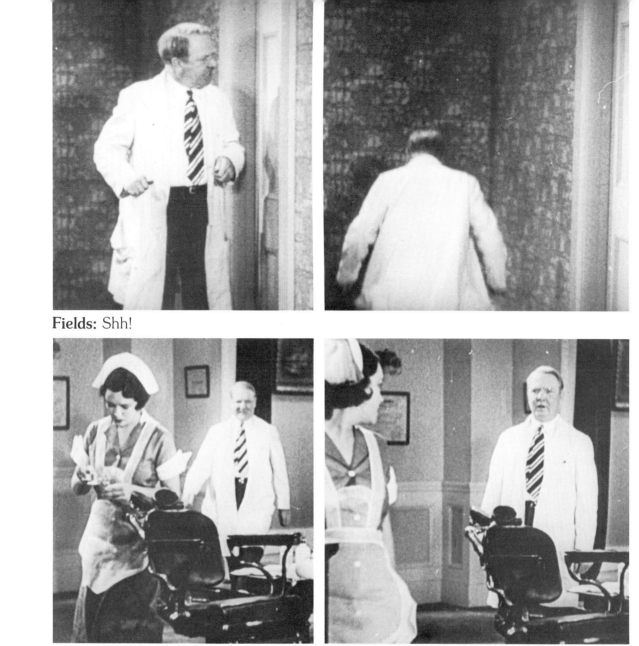

Fields: Shh!

Fields: Well, it won't be long now.

Fields: That female wrestler gone?
Nurse: Yes, she's gone.

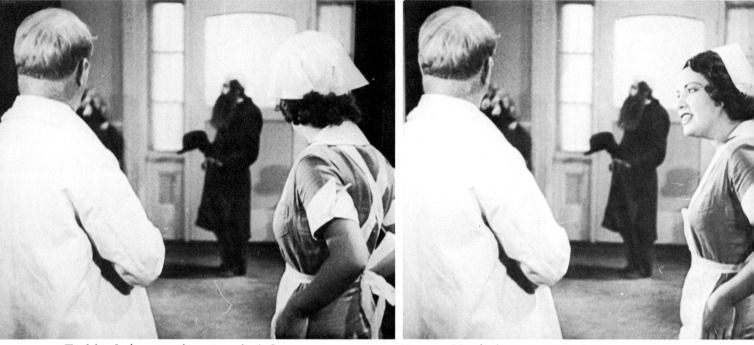

Fields: Is he standing in a hole?

Nurse: No, he's just a little fella.
Fields: Send him in, I'll fix him.

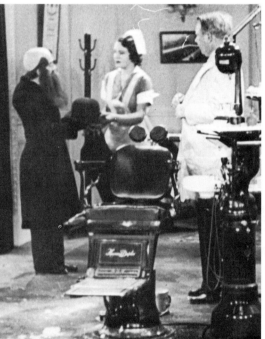

Nurse: This way, please.

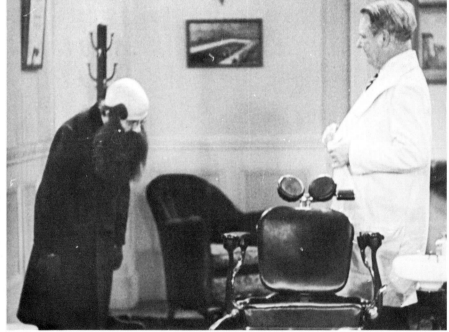

Fields: How do you do? How is *everything* in Moscow?

Fields:
Got two strikes on the boy there, eh?

Fields:
Sit down.

Fields:
Thank you.

113

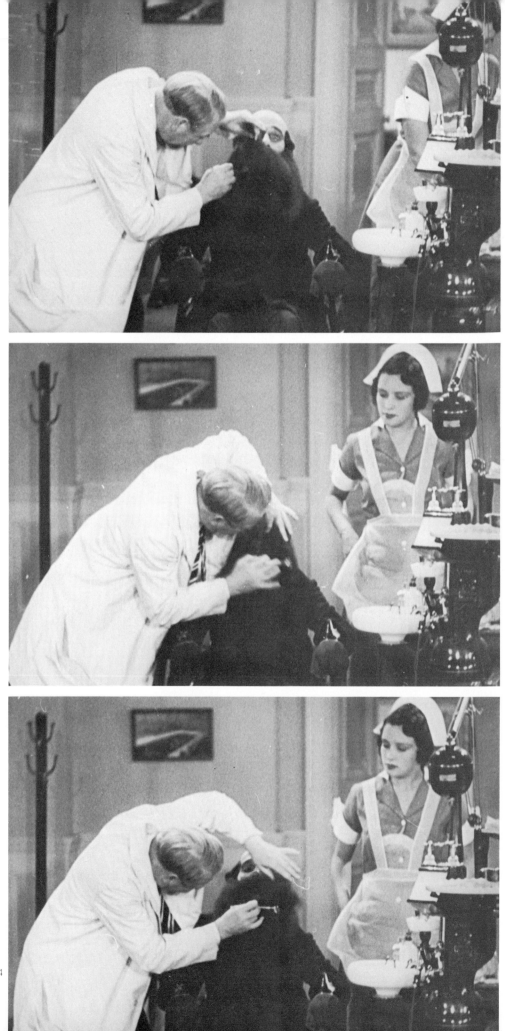

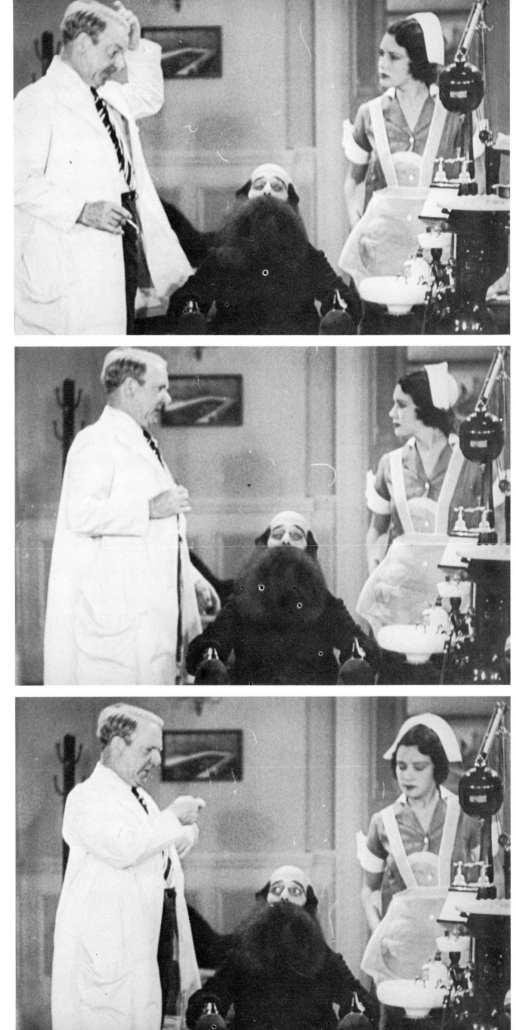

Fields:
I can't find his
mouth.

Fields:
Hand me that
stethoscope,
will you.
Thanks.

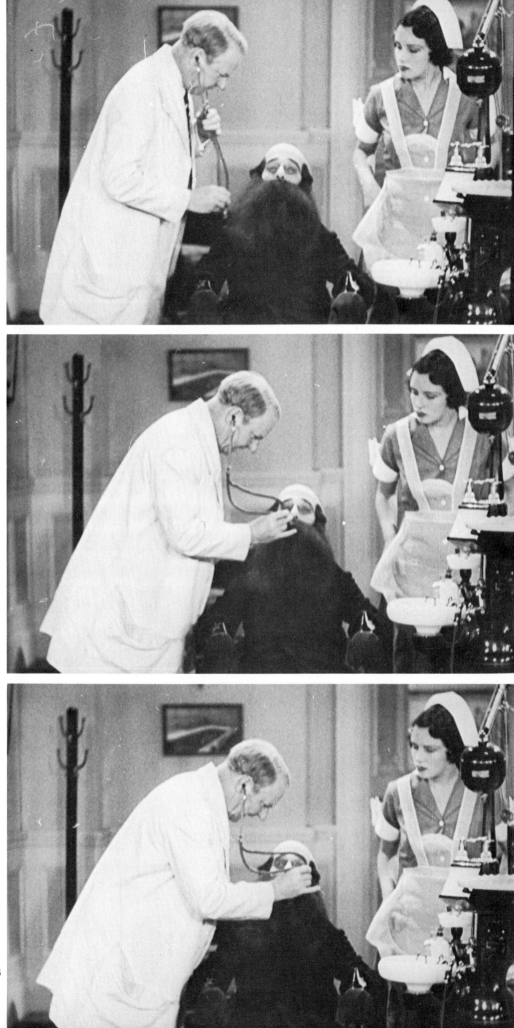

Fields:
Will you say 'Ah'?
Patient: Ah.

Fields:
Again.
Patient: Ah!

Fields:
Again.
Patient: Ah!

Fields:
I almost had it.
Patient: Ah!!

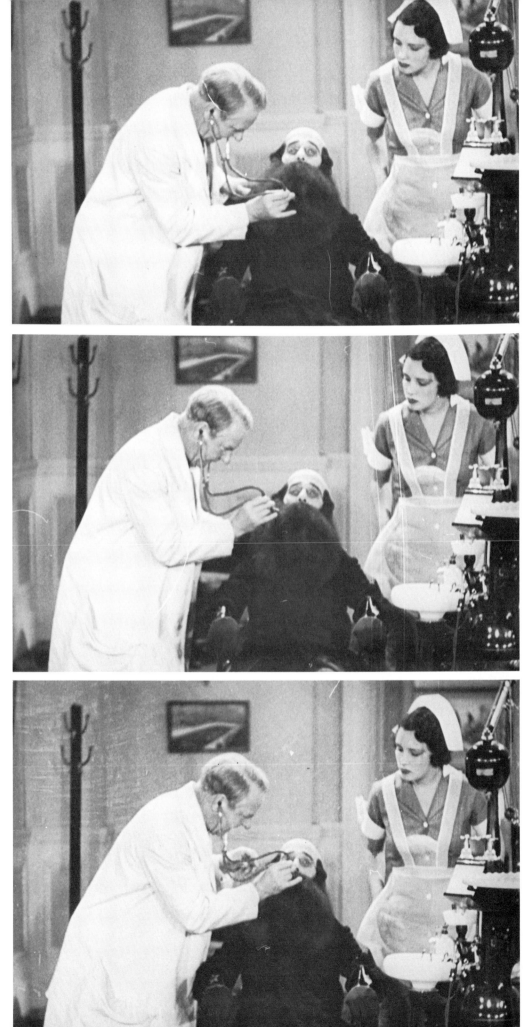

Fields:
Again, ah!

Fields:
There it is.

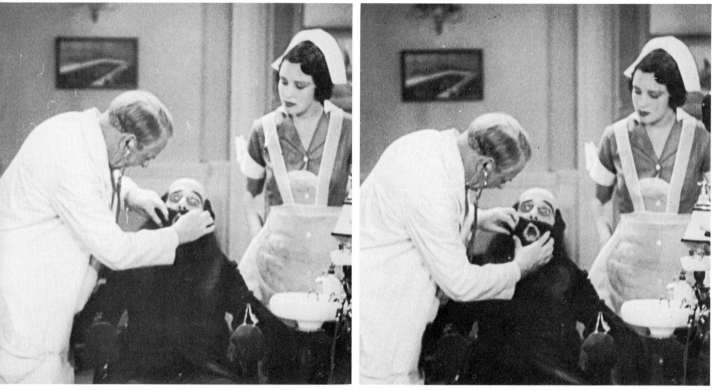

Fields: And a very pretty thing, too.

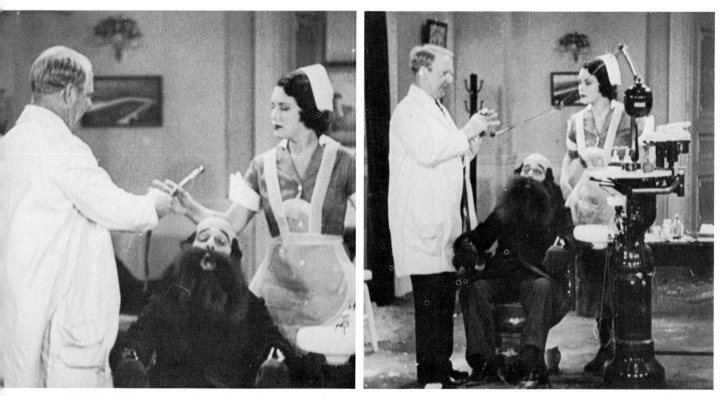

Fields: Let me see now, hand
me that drill. Thank you.

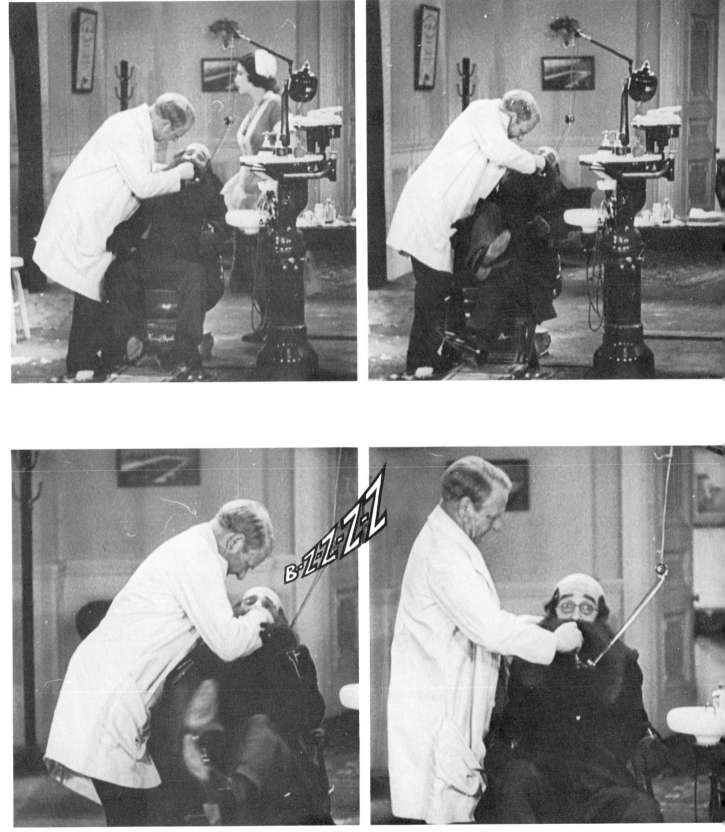

Fields: Now just open your mouth.

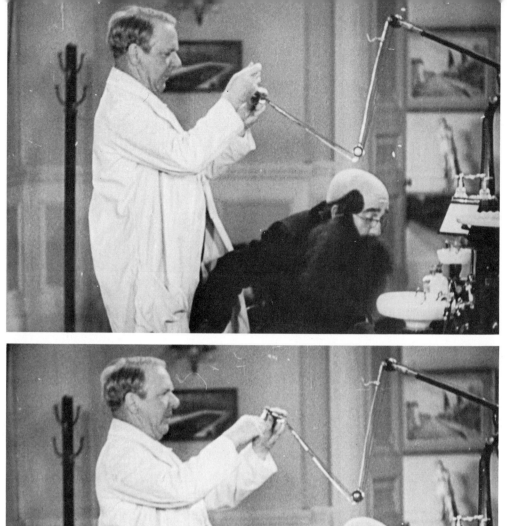

Fields:
OK., Can't say that
hurt you!

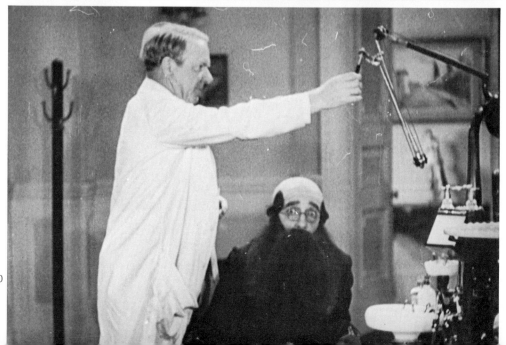

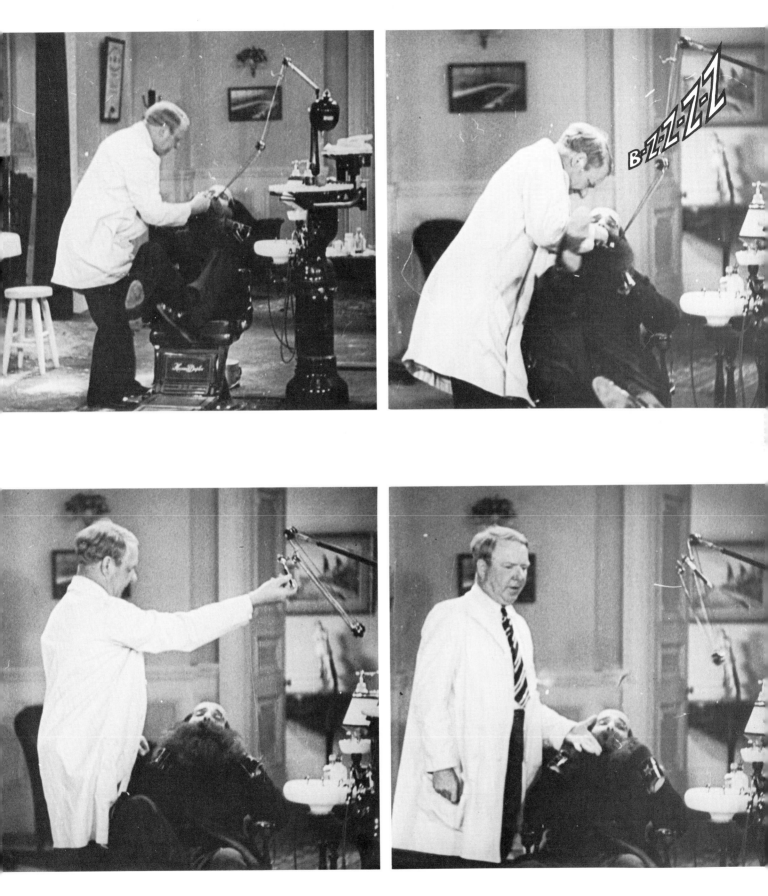

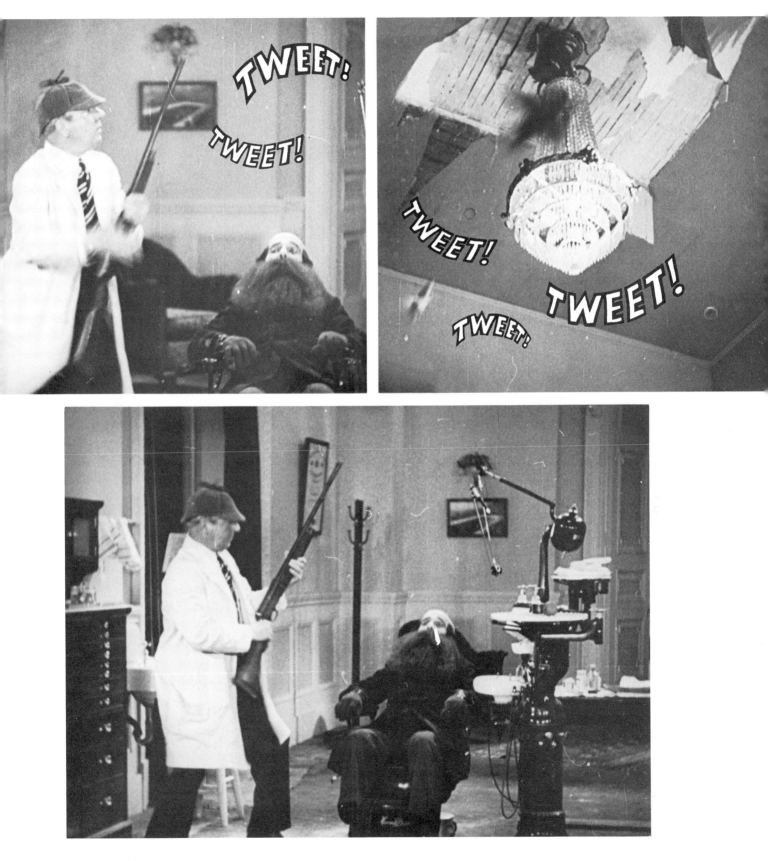

Nurse: Doctor, your daughter's going out with the ice man.

Fields:
No, she's not, I got her locked in her room.

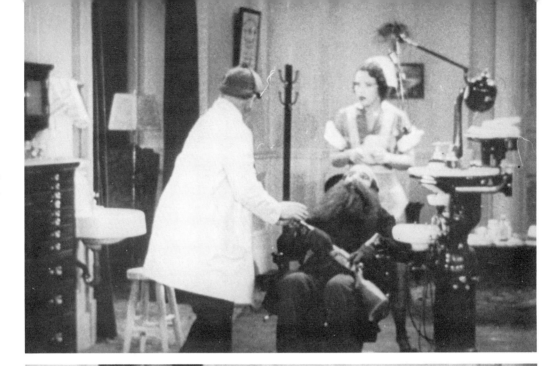

Nurse: But they're using a ladder.

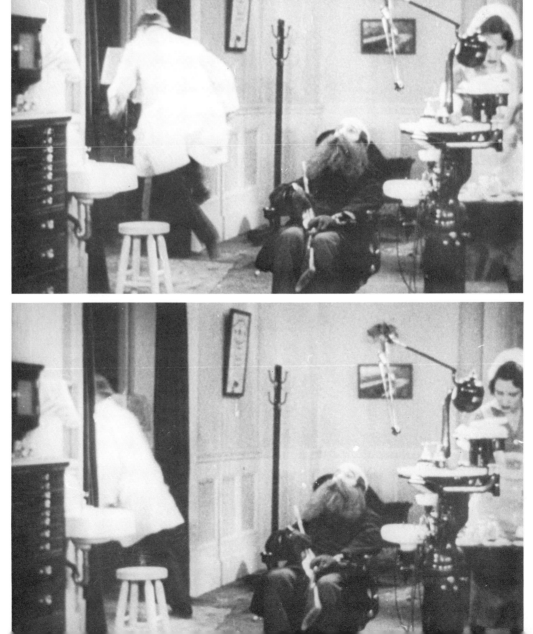

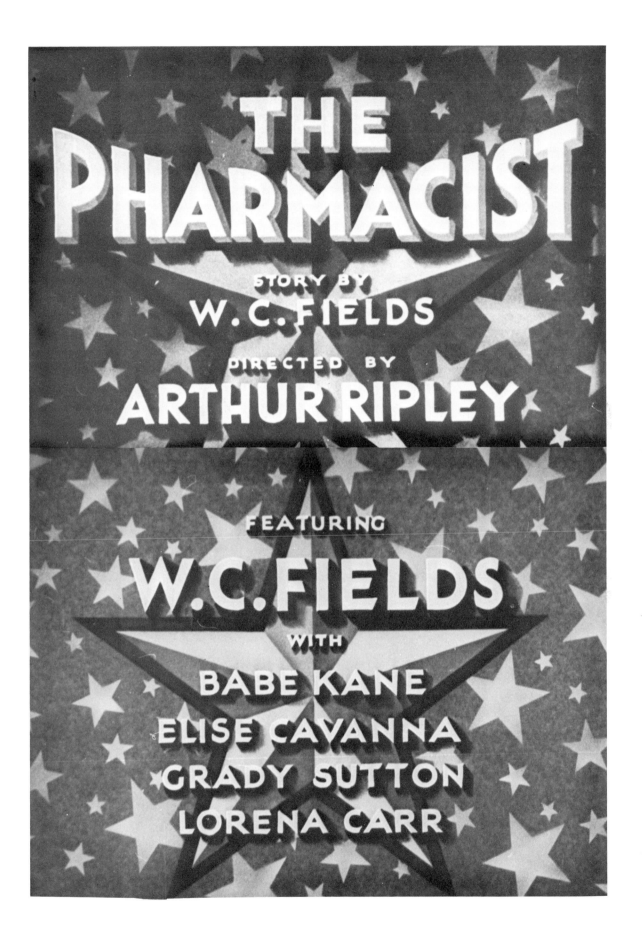

Wife: You'd better come up and get your dinner. Soup's on the table.

Fields: Coming right away, dear, coming right away.

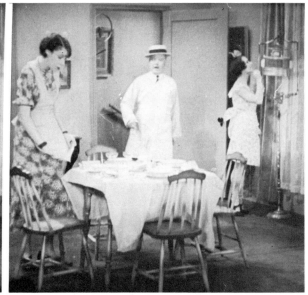

Fields: Where are the cocktails?

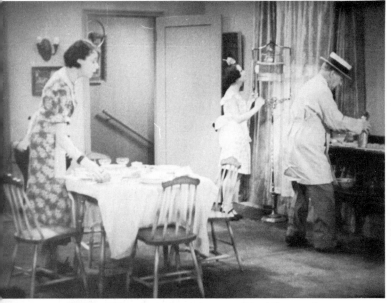

Wife: They're already mixed. All you have to do is put in the ice.

Daughter: Hello, Papa.

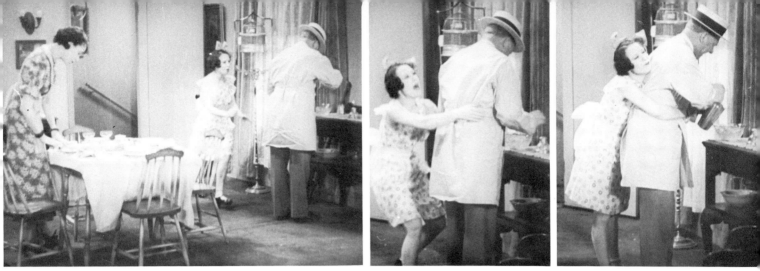

Fields: Hello dear.

Fields: Don't do that.

Fields: I've told you to stop it!

Daughter: What's the matter, don't you love me?

Fields: Certainly I love you.

Wife: What are you doing?

Fields: Well, she's not gonna tell me I don't love her!

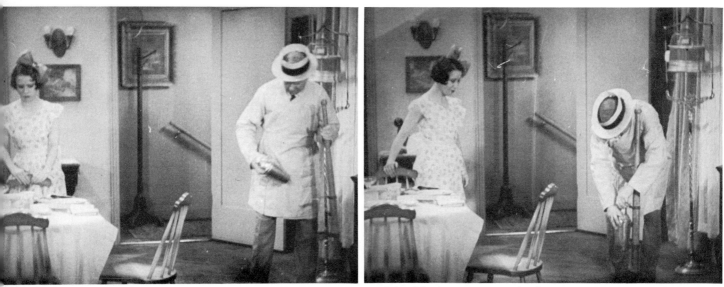
Fields: Here, want to play?

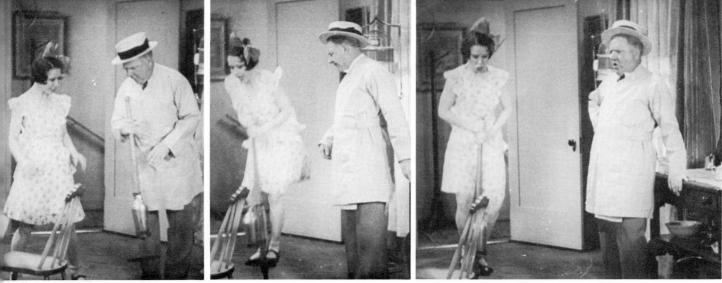
Daughter: Oh goody!

Fields: Say, remind me to order some more stamps tomorrow, will you.

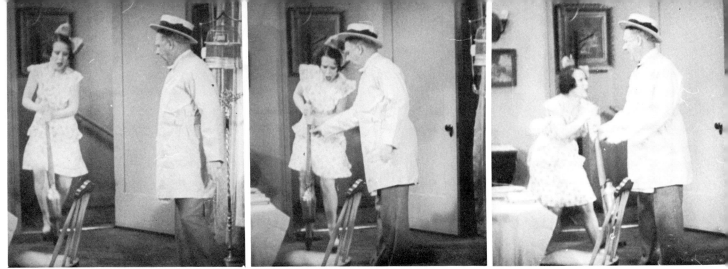

Fields: That's fine, that's fine.　　　**Fields:** That's fine, that's fine.

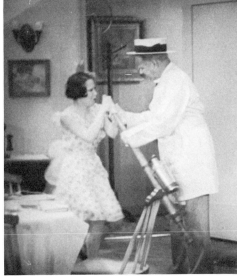

Fields: That's enough.

Fields: Let go, will you!

Daughter: Oh, let me do it just a minute, Pop.

Fields: Listen, will you stop it!

Daughter: Gee, I want to do it!

Fields: Is Papa's little angel going to sit down?

Fields: Won't Papa's little doll-baby sit down?

Fields: Or will Papa bust your sconce . . .

Wife: What do you mean, have you gone crazy?

Wife: Sit down and behave yourself!

Daughter: Gee whiz!—

Daughter: Mom, what's technocracy?

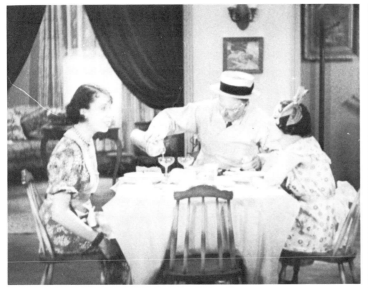

Wife: Ask your father, dear.

Daughter: Pop, what's technocracy?

Fields: Yes, dear, yes, er, eh, say, will you eat your soup and stop asking silly questions—

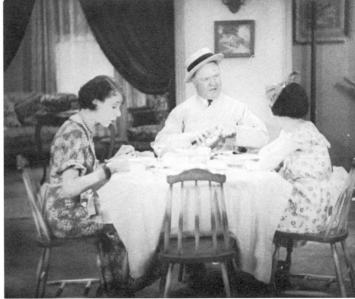

Fields: And stop that!

133

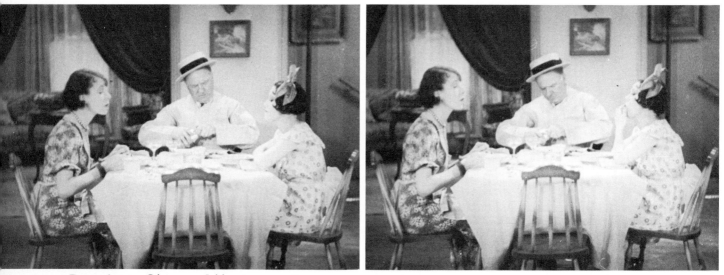

Daughter: Oh, gee, I like to pop it.

Fields: One more pop
and I'll pop you in the eye.

Fields: Now I have a chewing gum olive there in my martini!

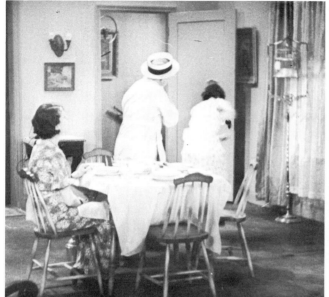

Fields: Get out of here!

Daughter: Gee, I'm hungry.

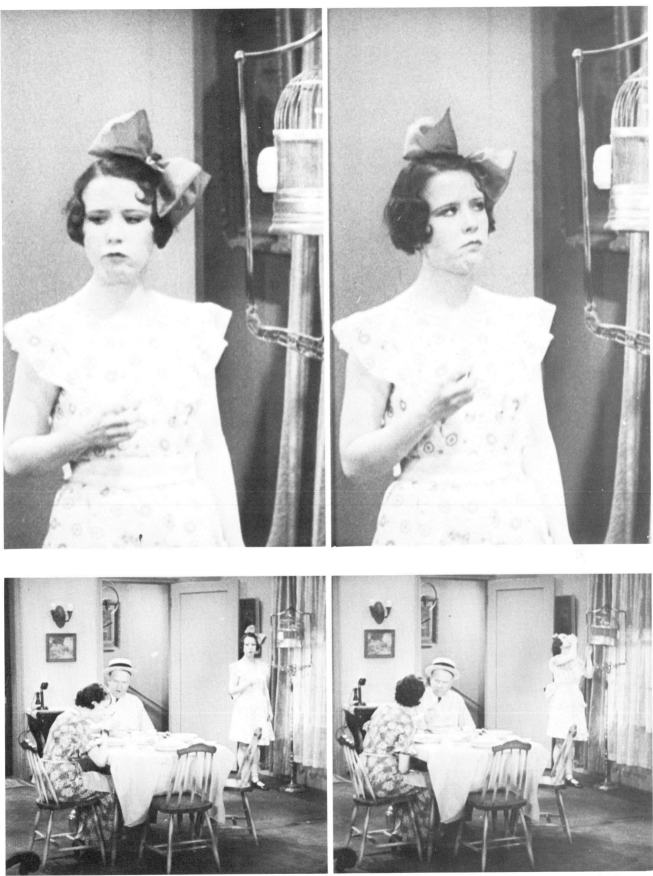

Fields: Why don't you learn that kid some manners?

Wife: Teach, my dear, teach. And it might be a good example if you would take your hat off.

Fields: I have hayfever. Another thing is that there's no top on it, so that don't matter.

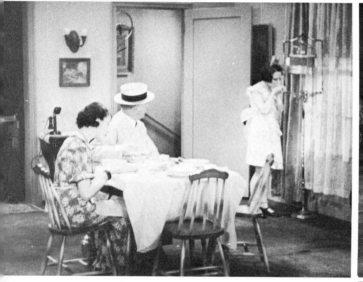

Fields: She ate the canary bird!!

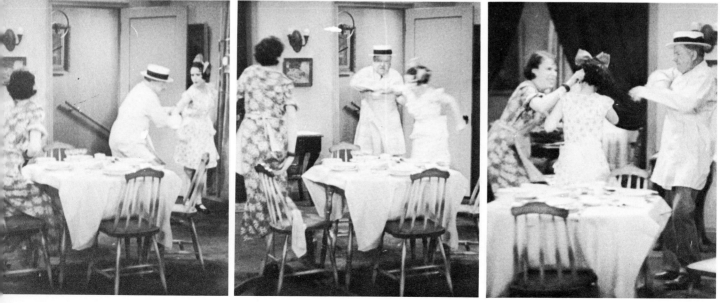

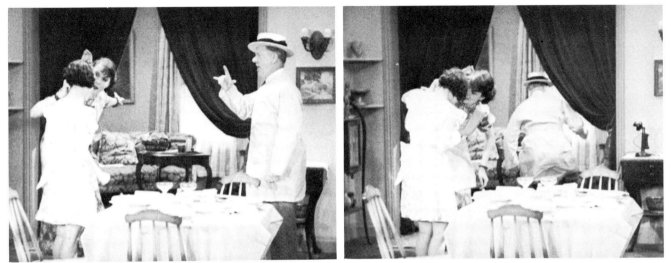

Wife: Get into that room!
Fields: Wait a minute—not yet!

Daughter: My ear!

Wife: Go over there and behave yourself!

Daughter: Oh, gee, Mom, it was just a little bird, and he hit me. Why don't you pick on somebody your own size?

Wife: Don't be insolent to your father.

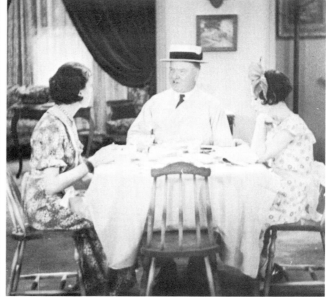

Fields: Ha, you should have seen me down at the firehouse, wrestling with the firemen. I picked six or eight of them and threw them over my head backwards...

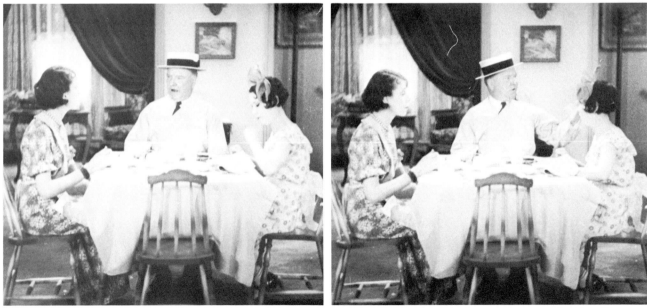

Fields: . . . well, three anyway.   **Fields:** Who taught that parrot to do that?

141

Fields: Stop it, stop it, stop it.

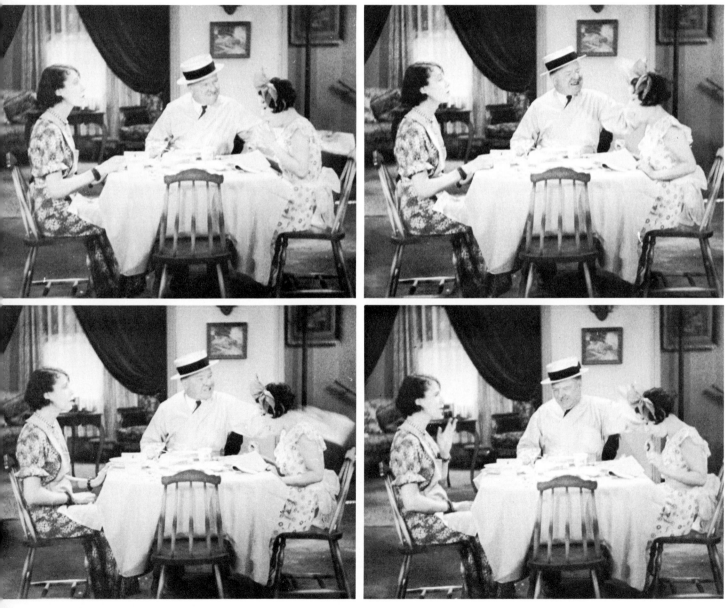

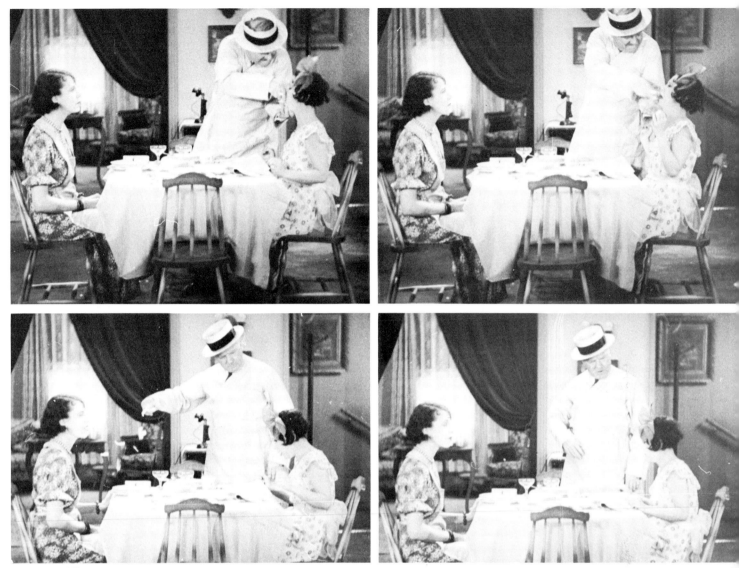

Fields: What did you want to eat a
canary bird for, anyway?

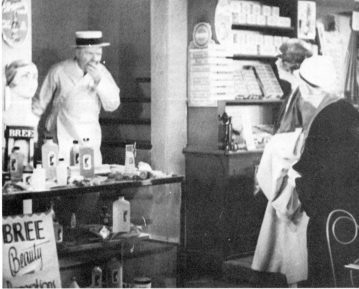

Fields: How do you do?

Woman: How do you do?

Woman: Is there a lady in attendance here?
Fields: Eh?

Woman: Is there a lady in attendance here?

Fields: Oh, yes, yes, yes, yes, yes, yes.
She'll be right down.

Fields: Hurry up downstairs, there are two ladies down there. They won't let me wait on them, they want a lady to wait on them.

Wife: Oh, I simply can't go down looking the way I am! What do they want?
Fields: They won't tell me what they want.

Daughter: I'll go down, Pop.
Fields: You sit down and eat your spinach.

Fields: Will you hurry up down!
Wife: If I have to serve in the drugstore I'll have to simply get some decent looking clothes first.

Fields: Hurry up down, dear, or we're going to lose their trade.

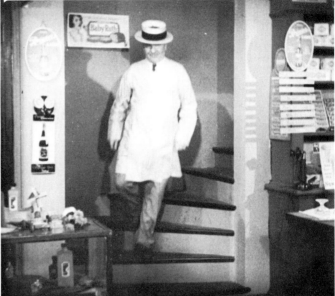

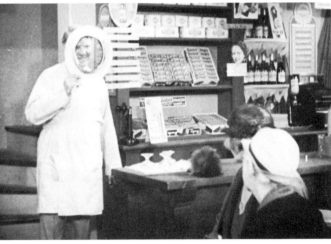

Fields: She'll be down in half a moment.

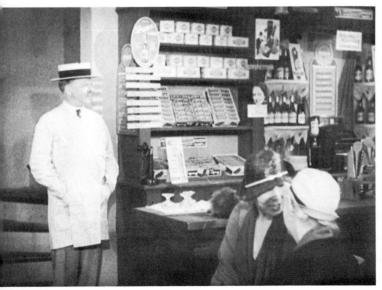

Fields: There's "Mother India." —

Fields: "Sex Life of the Polyp." —

Fields: "The Rover Boys in Youth." —

Fields: Cake à la mode? —

Fields: Rather an amusing little beggar.

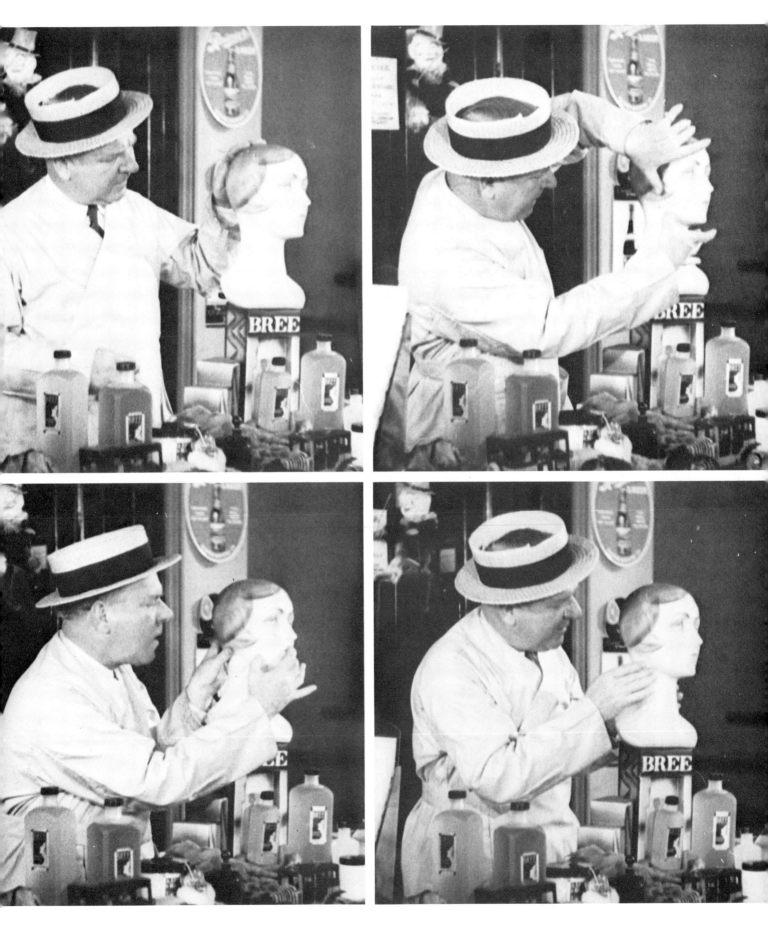

Fields: —Just a little black spot, that's all.—

Fields: Old Moscow in Winter. —

Fields: Can I interest you in a stamp?   **Customer:** Yeah, give me a stamp.

Fields: All right.

Customer: No, give me a purple one.

Fields: I'm sorry, we haven't any purple ones. I could paint one for you.

Customer: I don't want a painted one. A person hasn't got any rights in this country anymore.

Customer: The government even tells you what color stamps you've got to buy. That's the Democratic Party for you!

Fields: I've written to Washington about it.

Customer: What do you want to write to Washington for? He's dead.

Customer: —How much are your stamps?
Fields: Three cents.
Customer: All right—give me one.

Fields: O.K.
Customer: No, don't give me that dirty one, give me a clean one.

Customer: Give me the one out of the middle.

153

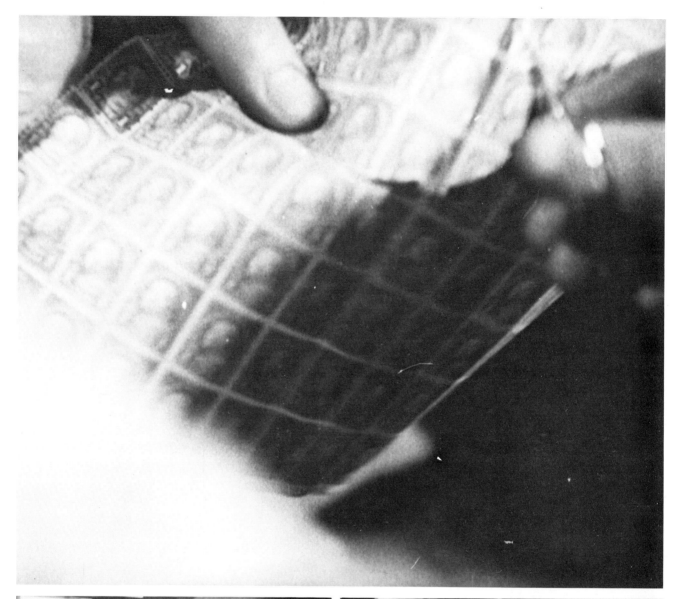

Fields: Sorry to keep you waiting —
I burnt my fingers.

Fields: Is that all right?
Shall we send it?

Customer: No, I'll take it along. —

Customer: Do you have change for a
hundred dollars?

Fields: No, I'm very sorry, I haven't.
Customer: Well, I'll pay you the next time I come in.

Fields: Oh, that's all right. Just a moment, just a moment.

Fields: We're giving these little souvenirs away today with every purchase.

Customer: Well, . . .

Woman: We won't be able to wait much longer.

Fields: Oh, ah, she'll be down, she'll be down, just half a sec, she'll be right down. She'll be right down.

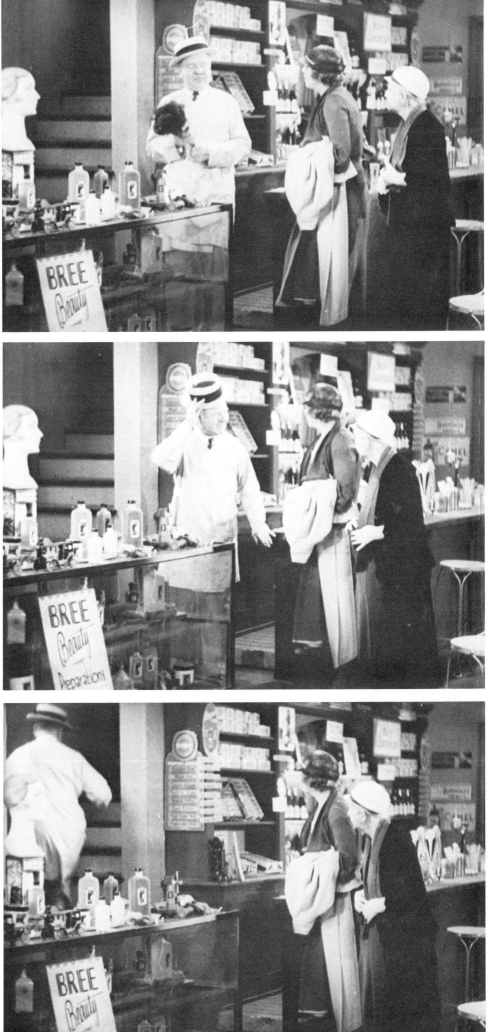

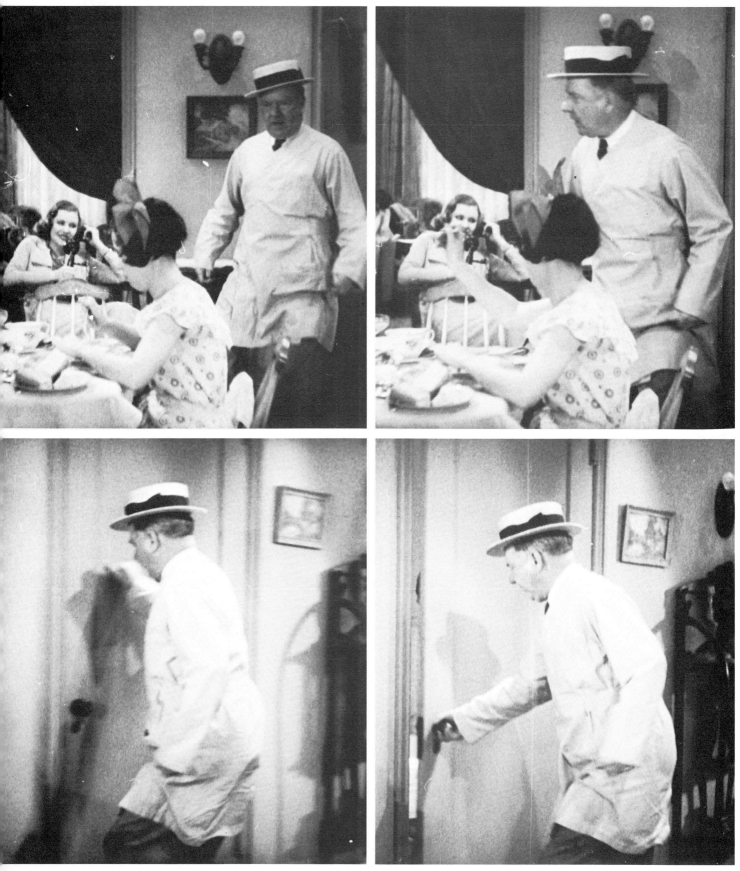

Wife: Close the door and get out of here. I'm putting on my gown.

Fields: Hurry up! Those ladies are getting very impatient. We're going to lose their trade!

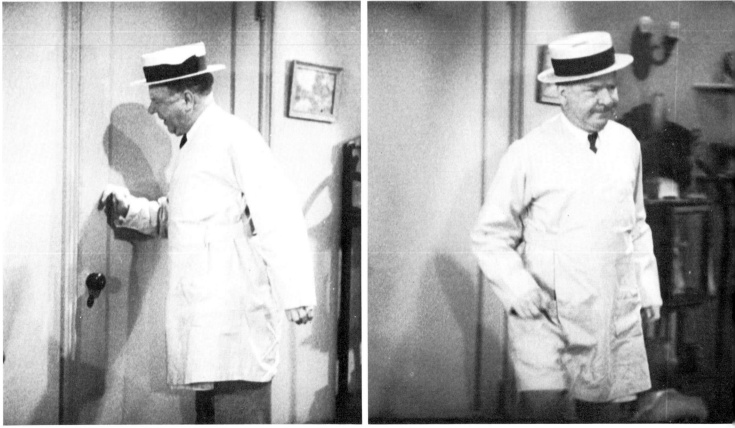

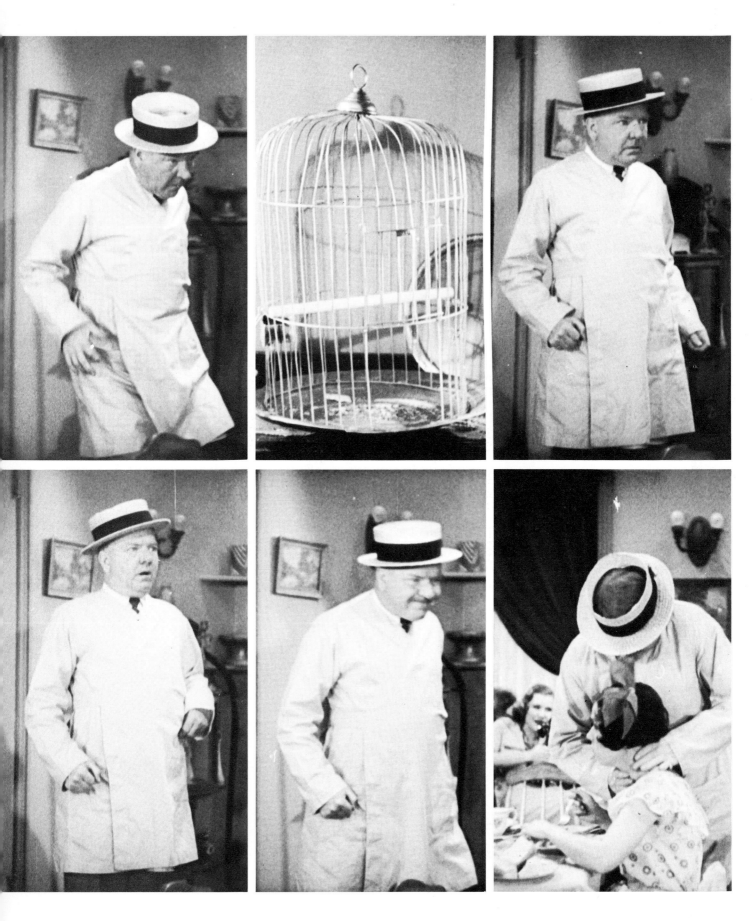

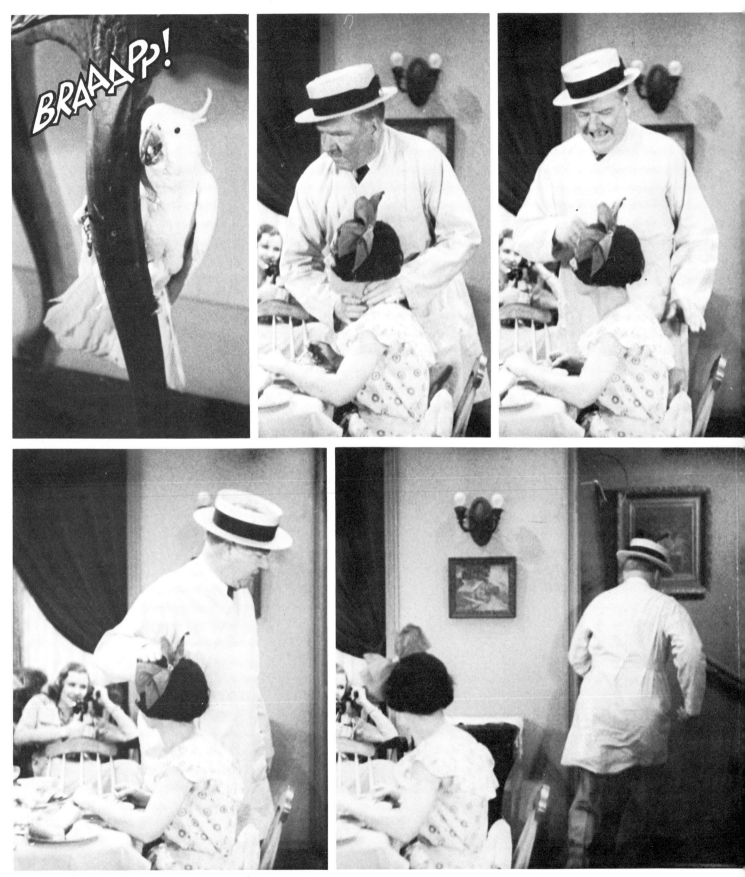

Fields: That's right, eat your spinach.

Fields: She'll be right down now.

Wife: What can I do for you?

Woman: Is there a ladies, restroom here?

Wife: Yes, right over there. The first door on your left.

Woman: Thank you.

Wife: You fool, why didn't you tell them?
Fields: They didn't ask me anything about it. It's not my fault, they didn't tell me.

Fields: How're you gonna know...

Fields: How do you do. What can I do for you?—

Fields: Certainly not.

Fields: Do you think
I'd break the laws of this
great, grand and glorious
United States of ours, just to
satisfy your depraved taste?
A thousand no's.

Fields: I've never had or sold a bottle of liquor since I've opened this place.

Plainclothesman: No? Well, you're not fooling me. I'll get you yet!

Fields: Well, maybe, and maybe not.

"And it ain't a fit night out for man or beast."

The Barber Shop

DIRECTED BY

ARTHUR RIPLEY

STORY BY W.C. FIELDS

FEATURING

W.C. FIELDS

WITH

ELISE CAVANNA

HARRY WATSON

DAGMAR OAKLAND

JOHN ST. CLAIR

CYRIL RING

Passer-by: Those sure were great fights last night, O'Hare.

O'Hare (Fields): Yes, they were. Never saw a better fight in my life.

Passer-by: I got a kick out of them myself.

O'Hare: So did I, so did I. When I see a fight like that, I feel like getting back into condition

O'Hare: and getting into the fight game myself.

O'Hare: Ah, that's better.

Man: Hello, O'Hare, what do you know?

O'Hare: Not a thing, not a thing.

O'Hare: That lug tells his wife everything he knows.

Woman: Good morning, Mr. O'Hare.

O'Hare: Oh, good morning, Mrs. Scroggin.
How's Mr. Scroggin?
Woman: He's not so well this morning.

O'Hare: Oh, that's unfortunate. I'm sorry to hear that.
Woman: I'm worried about him.

O'Hare: Well, I am, too.

O'Hare: He was out on one of his benders last night again. How one can drink all that raw alcohol I'll never know.

O'Hare: Fine man he is!

O'Hare: Get out, get out, get out of here, get out of here, get out of here, get out of here.

O'Hare: You think all I got to do all day long is paint that pole?

O'Hare: How do you do, sir.

O'Hare: Sit down.

Manicurist: Manicure?
Customer: No.

O'Hare: Hair cut or shave?

Customer: Yeah.

175

O'Hare: I beg your pardon—isn't your name Sludge?
Customer: Yeah.

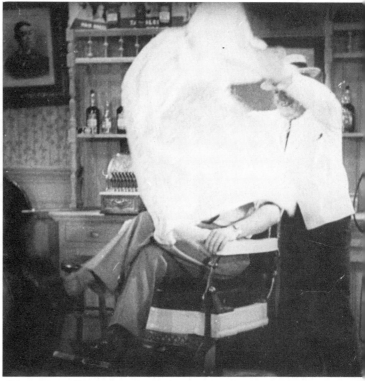

O'Hare: I thought so.

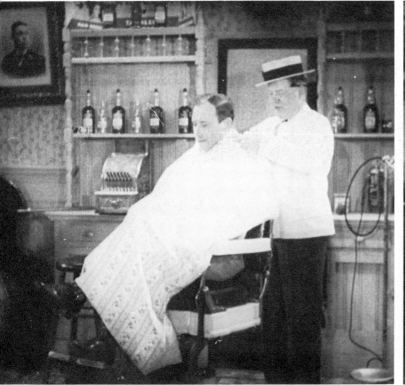

O'Hare: I didn't recognize your face when you first came in.

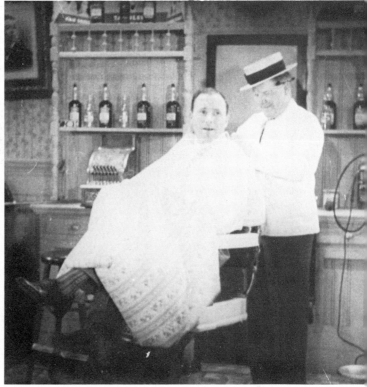

Customer: Now it's all healed up since I was in here last.

Manicurist: Oh, Mr. O'Hare, I see they're offering two thousand dollars reward for the bandit that robbed the bank in Cucamonga City.

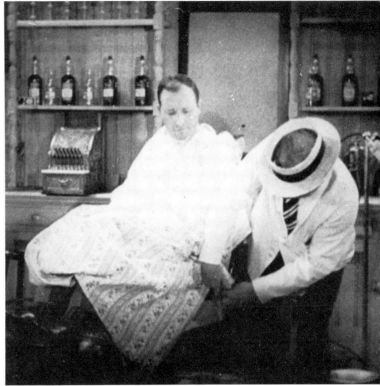

O'Hare: Two thousand dollars—

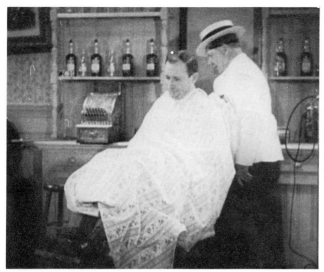

O'Hare: I'd like to get that fellow. If I wasn't so busy I'd go over and choke that guy to death;

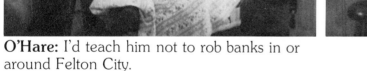

O'Hare: I'd teach him not to rob banks in or around Felton City.

O'Hare: drubbing . . . drubbing.

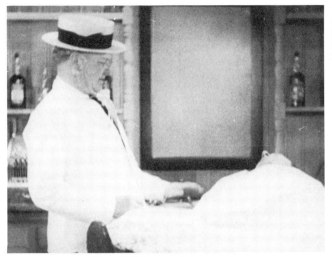

Manicurist: Mr. O'Hare, did you know you had your hat on backwards?

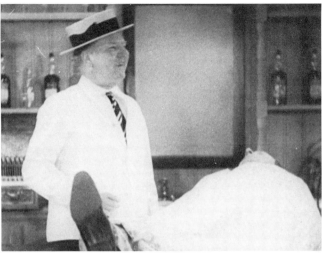

O'Hare: What, I beg your pardon?
Manicurist: Did you know you had your hat on backwards?

O'Hare: Oh, no—oh, thank you very much. I had it on backwards the day before yesterday,

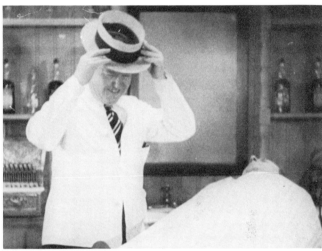

O'Hare: and a friend of mine came up

O'Hare: Drubbing, drubbing . . . drubbing . . . drubbing . . . drubbing . . . drubbing . . .

O'Hare: and kicked me in the stomach.—

Ronald: Hey, catch it, catch it—home run, home run!

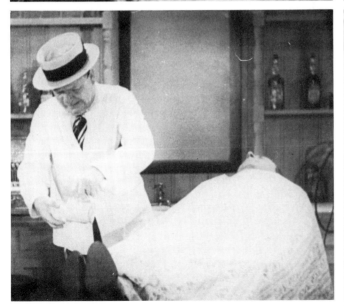

O'Hare: Be careful, boys, be careful.
Boys: We will, Mr. O'Hare.

O'Hare: I haven't thrown a spitball since I was first-line pitcher on the Baltimore Orioles years ago.

O'Hare: Look out, son—get out on the other side of the street!
Ronald: O.K.

O'Hare: There she goes!

Policeman: Ow!

O'Hare: Sorry. —

O'Hare: He wasn't hurt.—Drubbing...

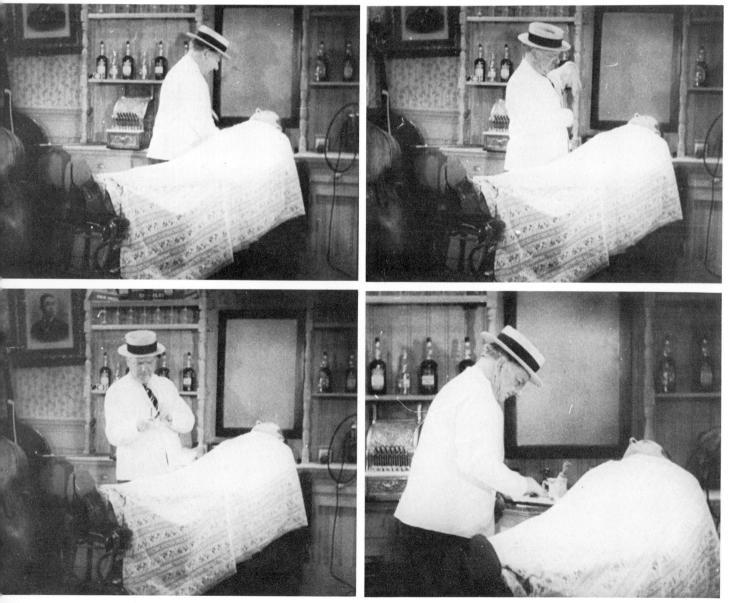

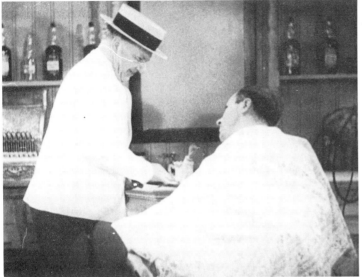

O'Hare: Just sharpening it . . . —

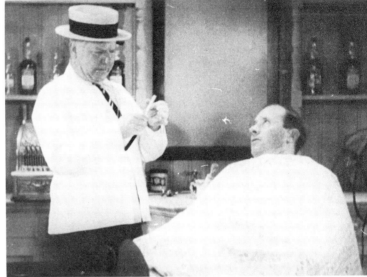

O'Hare: Shut your eyes, please.—

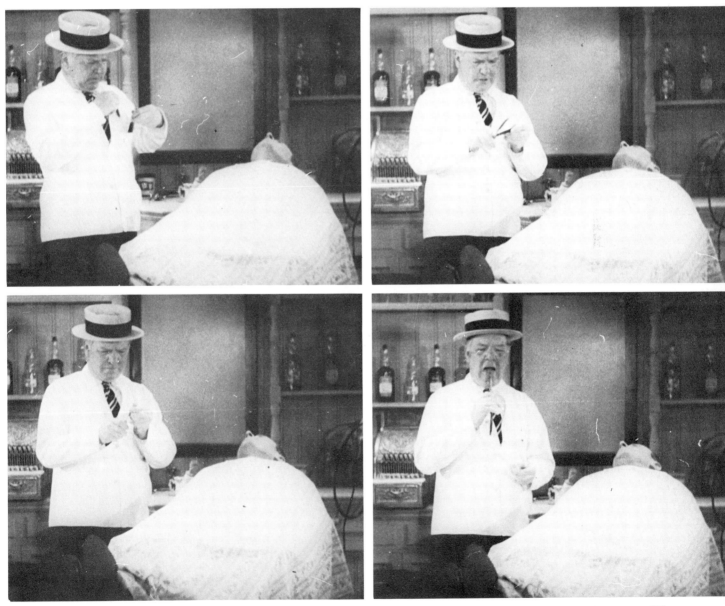

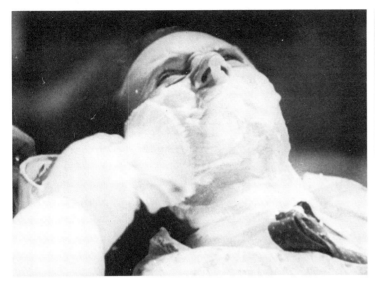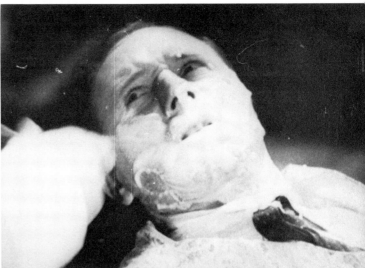

O'Hare: That tickle?—

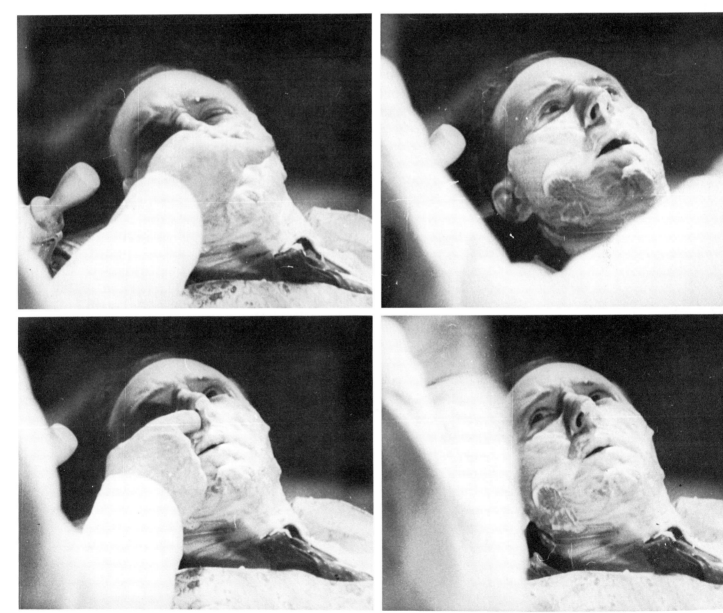

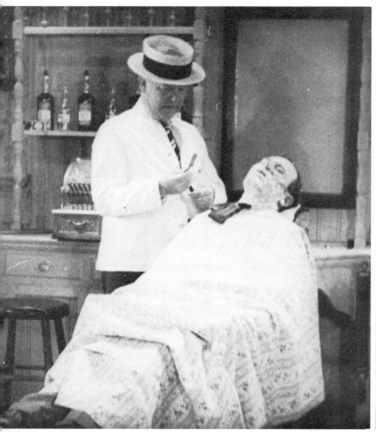

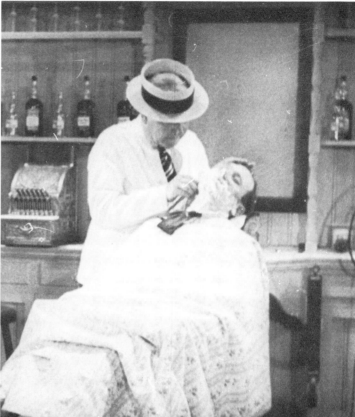

O'Hare: That won't hurt, that won't hurt.—

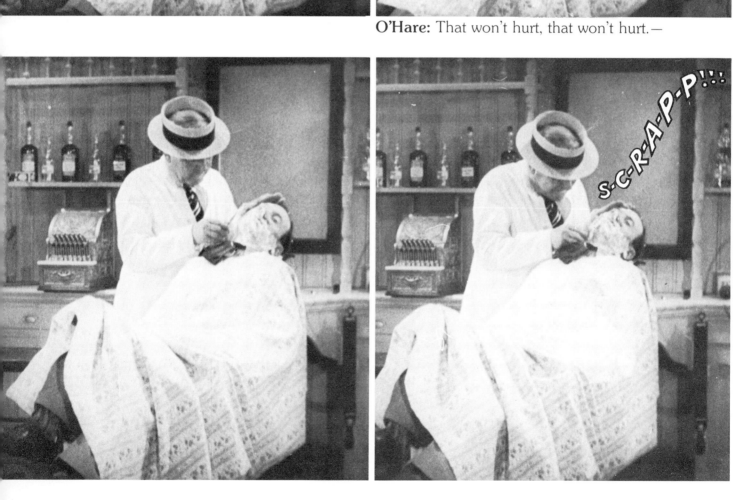

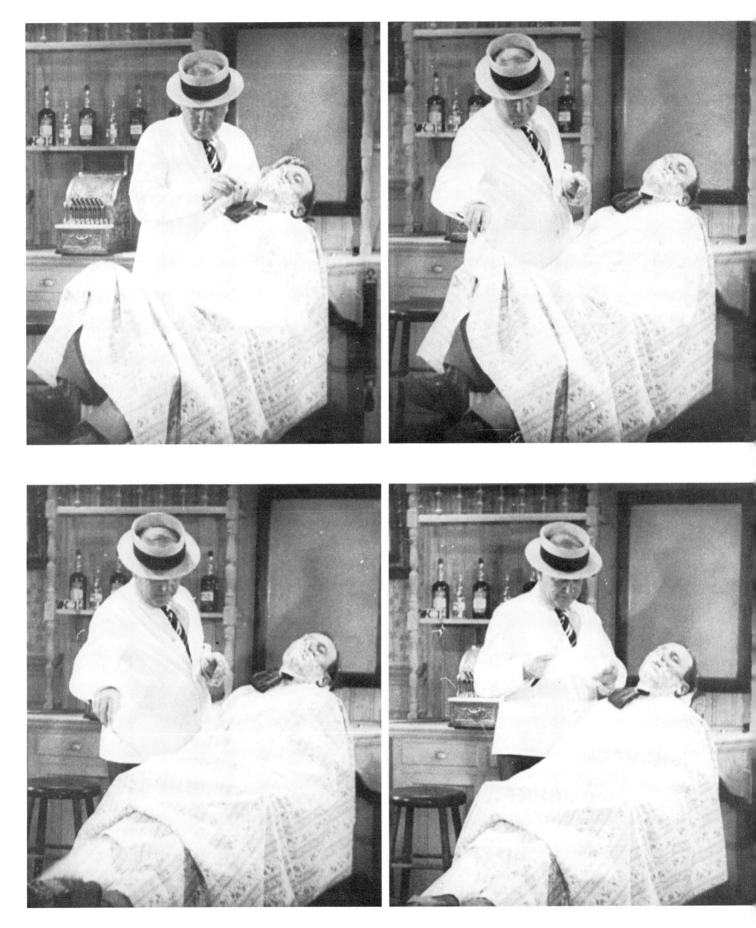

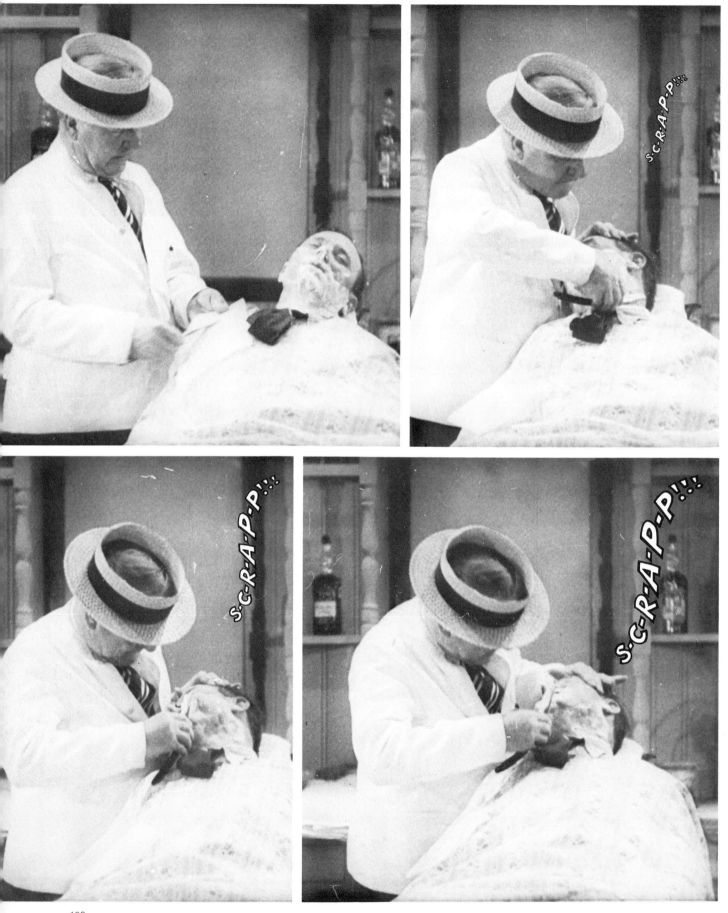

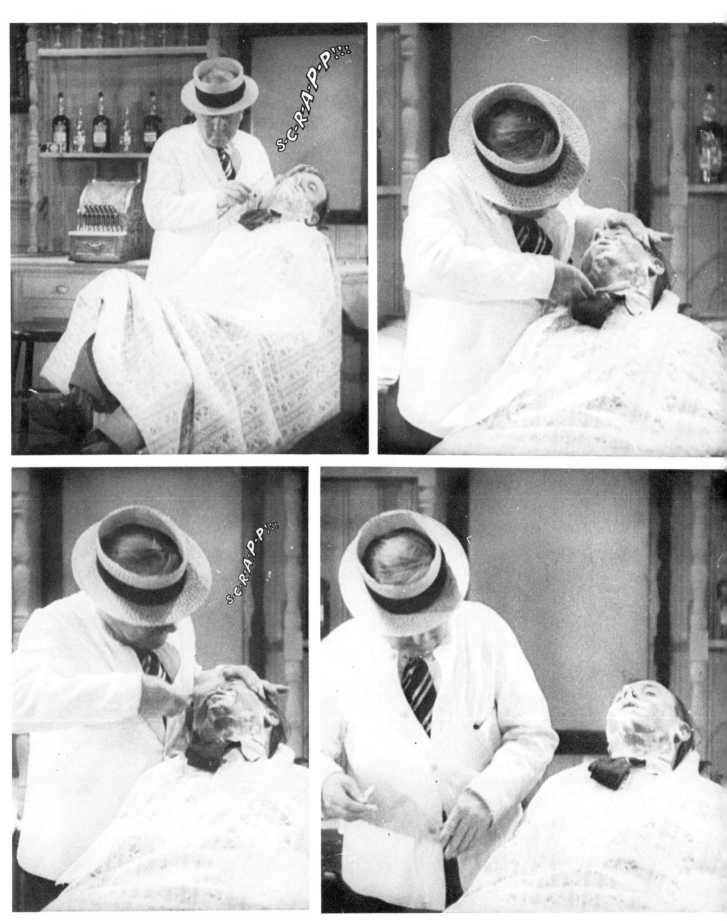

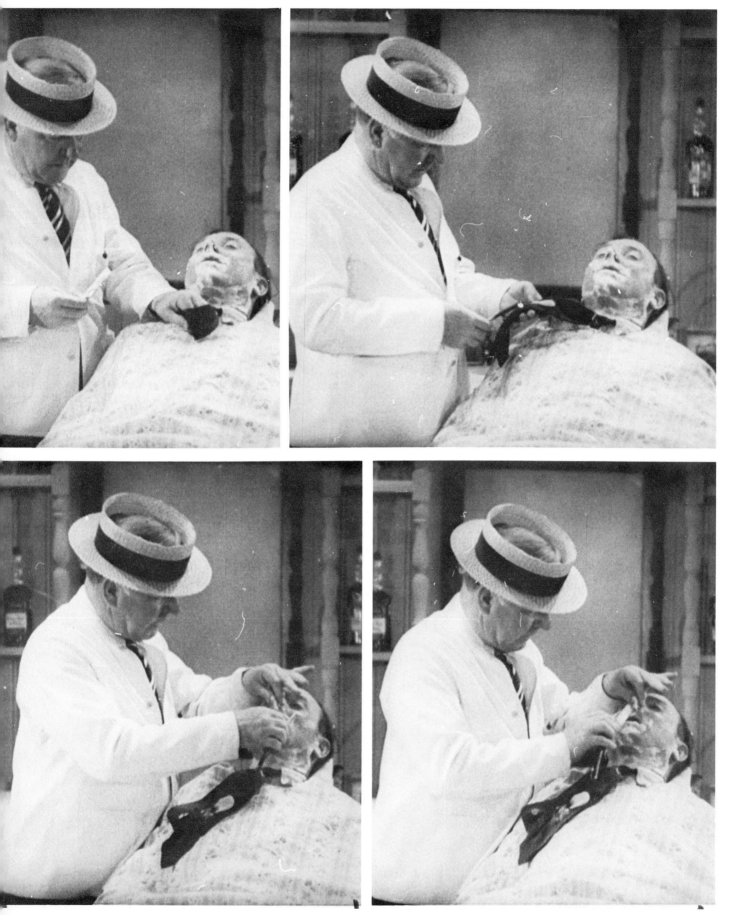

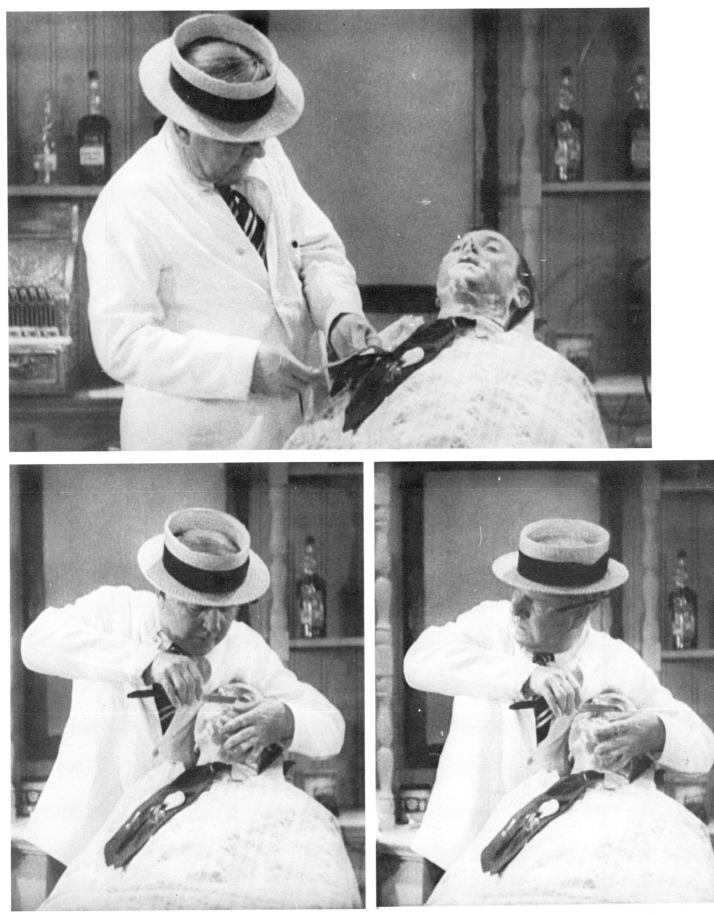

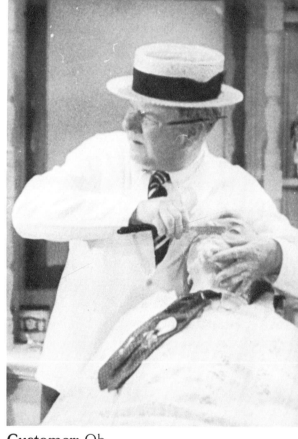

Customer: Oh—

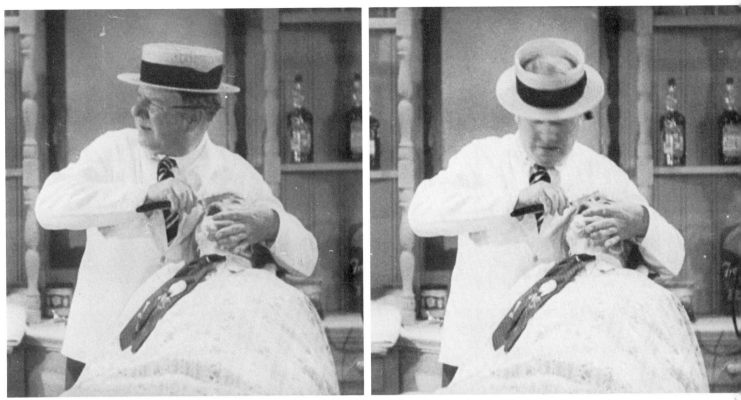

Customer: oh!

O'Hare: O.K., not your fault.

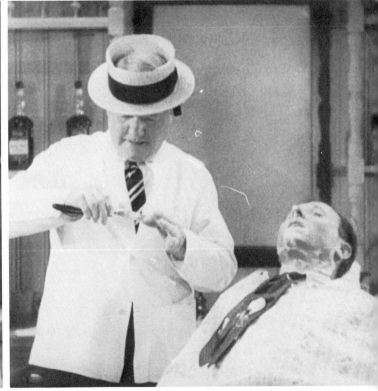

O'Hare: I'll fix that. No harm done, no harm done. —

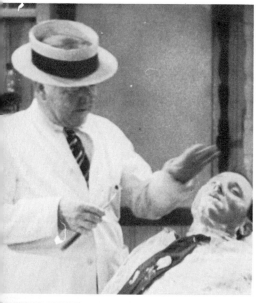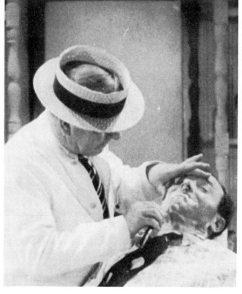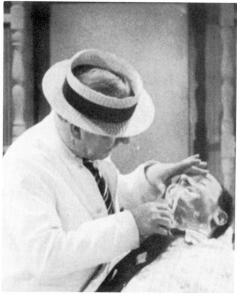

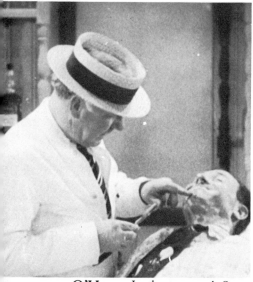

O'Hare: Is that a mole?   **Customer:** Yeah, I've had it all my life.

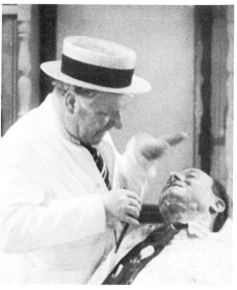

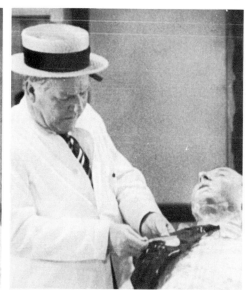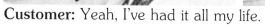

O'Hare: You don't have it anymore.

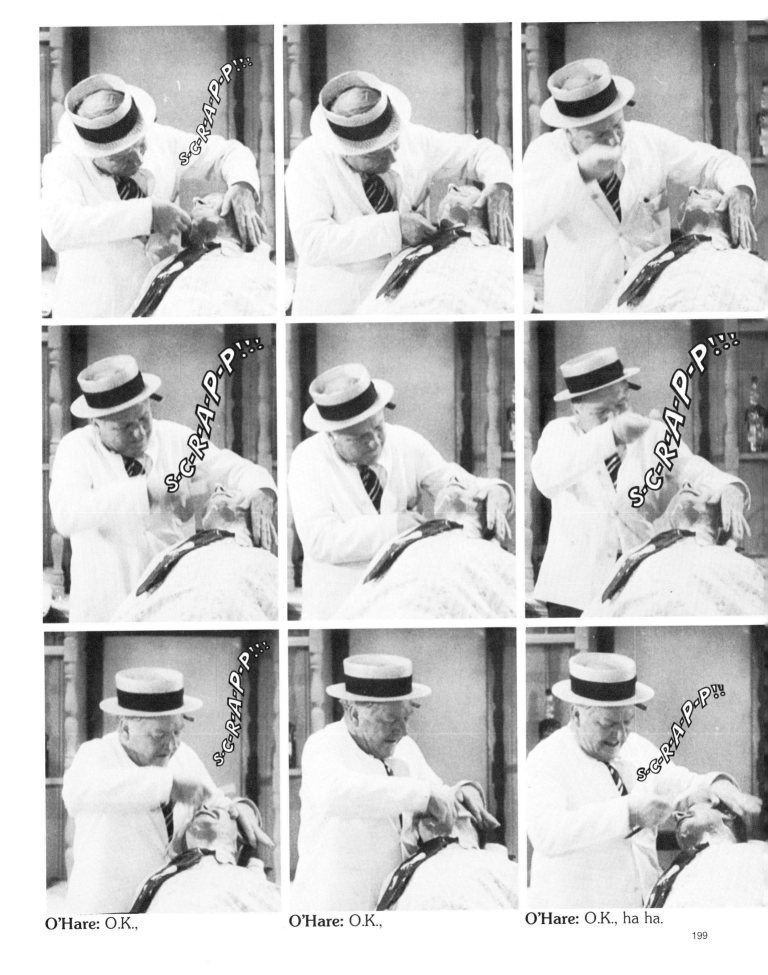

O'Hare: O.K.,

O'Hare: O.K.,

O'Hare: O.K., ha ha.

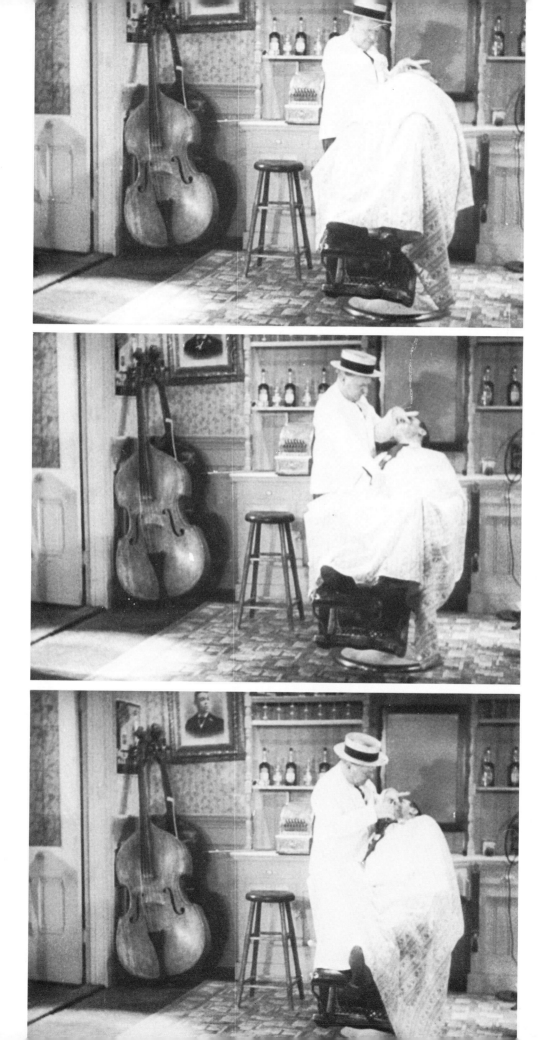

O'Hare: That's all right.

O'Hare: How do you do?

Fat man: How do you do. Is it true that you can take weight off with that steam of yours?

O'Hare: I positively guarantee it!

Fat man: My wife says if I don't shed some of this fat off of me, she'll leave me.

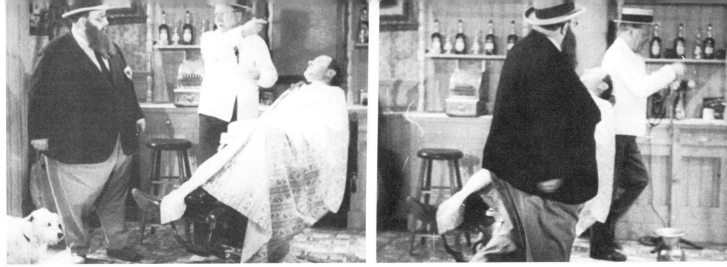

O'Hare: Step right this way.

O'Hare: Right in here, this room right here.

O'Hare: Just go in this hangar—change your clothes in there.

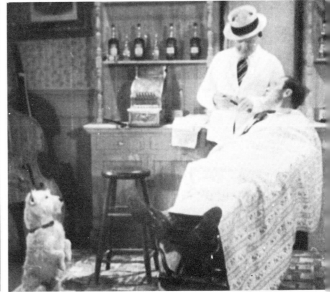

O'Hare: If he ever took his shoes off he'd go right up in the air!

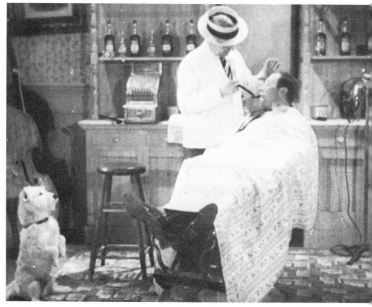

O'Hare: Oh, it's a very funny thing.

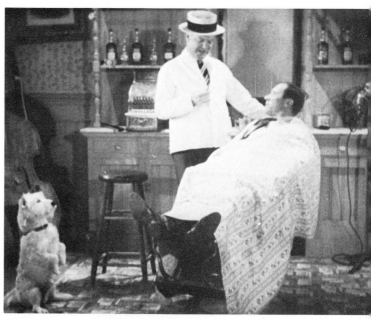

Customer: Say, what's that dog doing in here?

O'Hare: The other day, a man was in here, and I was shaving him. The razor slipped and I cut his ear off. The dog got it. Ever since he's been hanging around here waiting . . .

O'Hare: Go away, go away! Go get some other meat, you can't eat here.

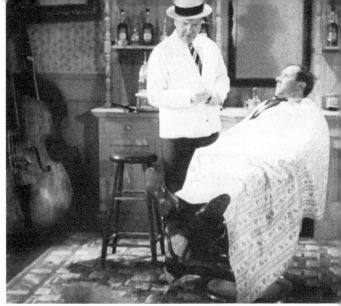

O'Hare: I don't have anything to do with that 'cute puppy' stuff. I just can't be very ethical with them.

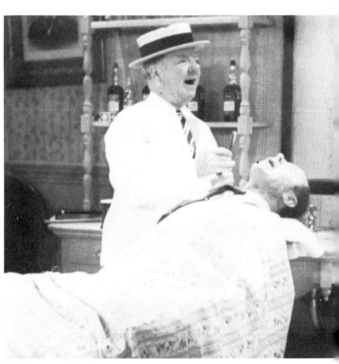

O'Hare: Ah, there you are—

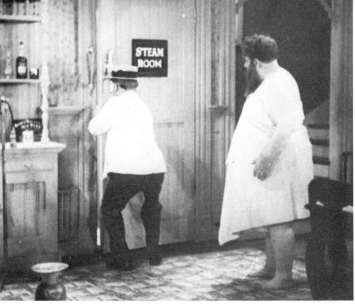

O'Hare: Here's the steam room,

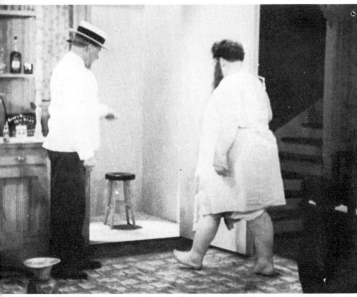

O'Hare: right in there, sit down.

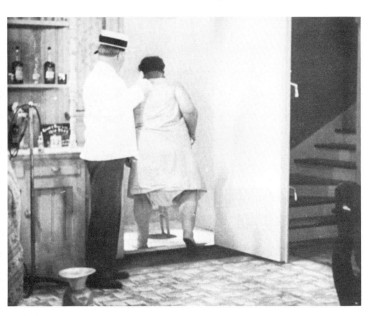

O'Hare: I'll turn the steam on right away.—

O'Hare: Come on, Ethel, get excited!

BOOM!

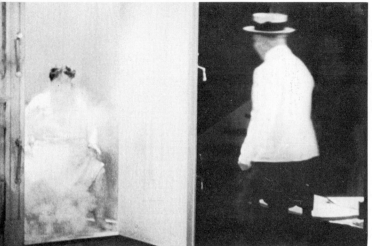

O'Hare: There you are. Now don't stay in there over a minute! If it gets too hot just press that button.

O'Hare: And the light will go on.

O'Hare: And if you're in any trouble just pull that rope and the horn will blow; up there.

O'Hare: And I'll get you right out.

O'Hare: He'll be there a minute and it will take a ton off him.

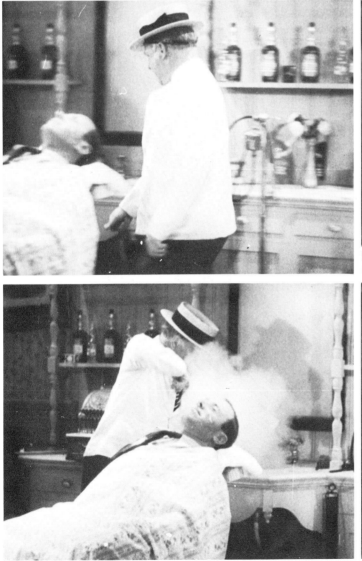

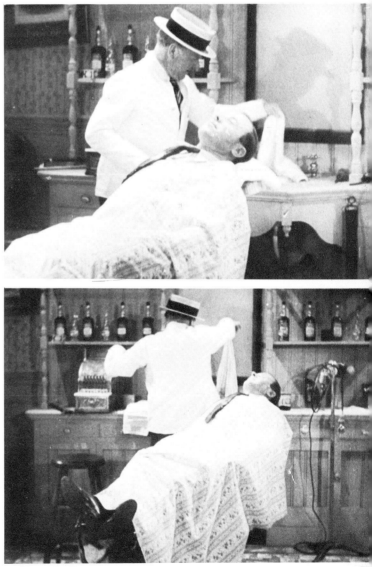

O'Hare: I'll give you a hot towel, and he'll be right through in there.—

 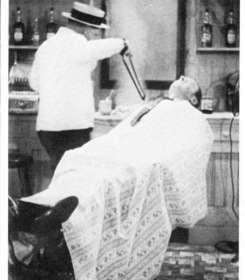 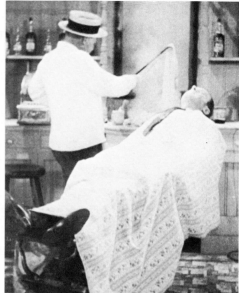

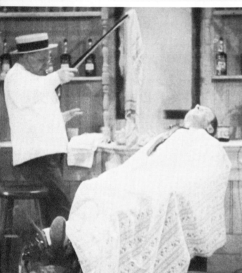 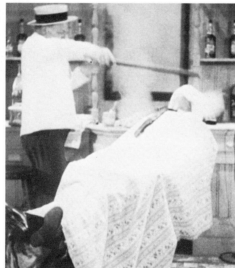 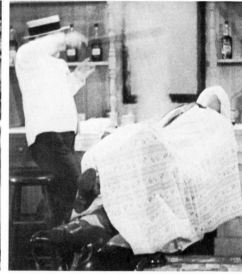

O'Hare: All right, all right, all

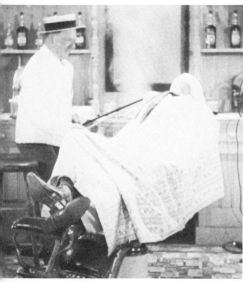  

O'Hare: right, all right,

O'Hare: all right, all right, all right, there you are.—

O'Hare: Police call!

O'Hare: They are after that bandit!

Manicurist: Which way did they go?

O'Hare: They went up that way.

O'Hare: You know, when I hear that old siren, I feel like an old fire-horse.

O'Hare: Want to get back in the harness again. I used to be a detective once.

Manicurist: Really, Mr. O'Hare?
O'Hare: Yeah, yeah.

Manicurist: You seem to have been everything!
O'Hare: I guess I was, I was . . .

Wife: Cornelius!

O'Hare: Yes? Yes, my little wisp?

Wife: Did you mail that letter I gave you yesterday morning?

213

O'Hare: Er, yes, er, er,

O'Hare: Yes,

O'Hare: Yes I did, dear, yes.
Manicurist: I think I'll go and have my dress made.

O'Hare: Yes, go ahead,

O'Hare: yes, that would be fitting.

214

Mrs. Broadbottom:
How do you do,
Mr. O'Hare.

O'Hare:
Fine, thank you.

Mrs. Broadbottom:
Would you
mind taking care
of the baby while I
go in the drugstore?

O'Hare: I'd love to,
I'd love to. How's Mr.
Broadbottom?

Mrs. Broadbottom:
Fine, thanks. I'll be
just a minute.

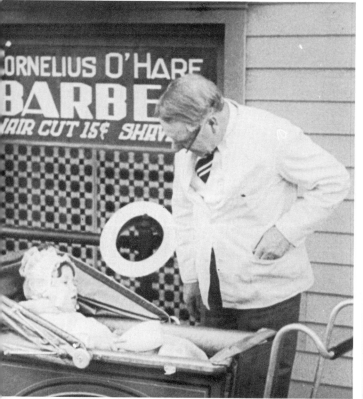

O'Hare: O.K. Here, kitchy, kitchy, come here. My little woolly-britches.

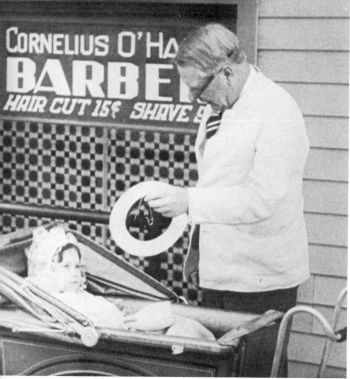

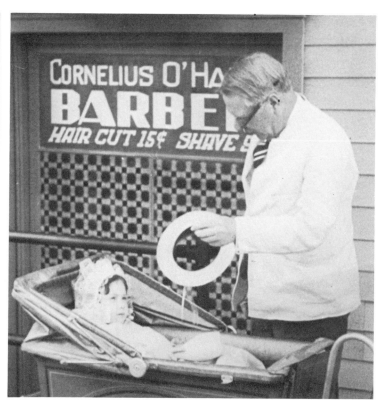

O'Hare: Don't you know that to swallow a thing like that can kill you?

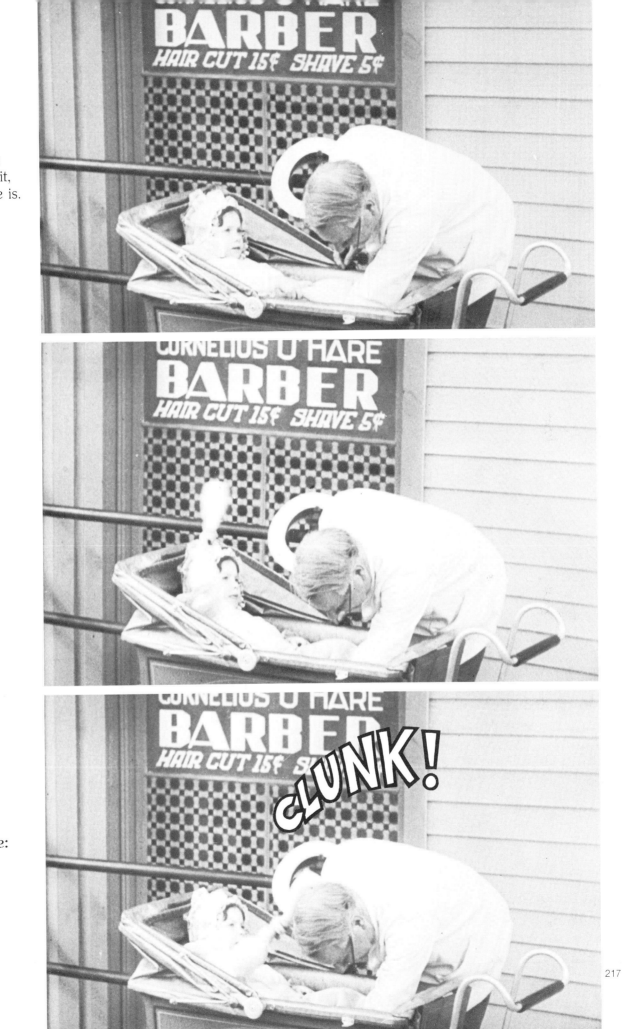

O'Hare:
I've got it,
here she is.

O'Hare:
Ow!—

CLUNK!

217

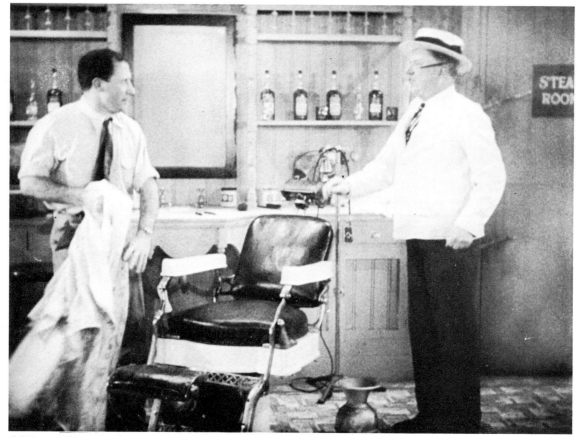

O'Hare: Wouldn't you like to wait for a little powder?

Customer: I'd like to have enough powder to blow you to smidgeons.

220

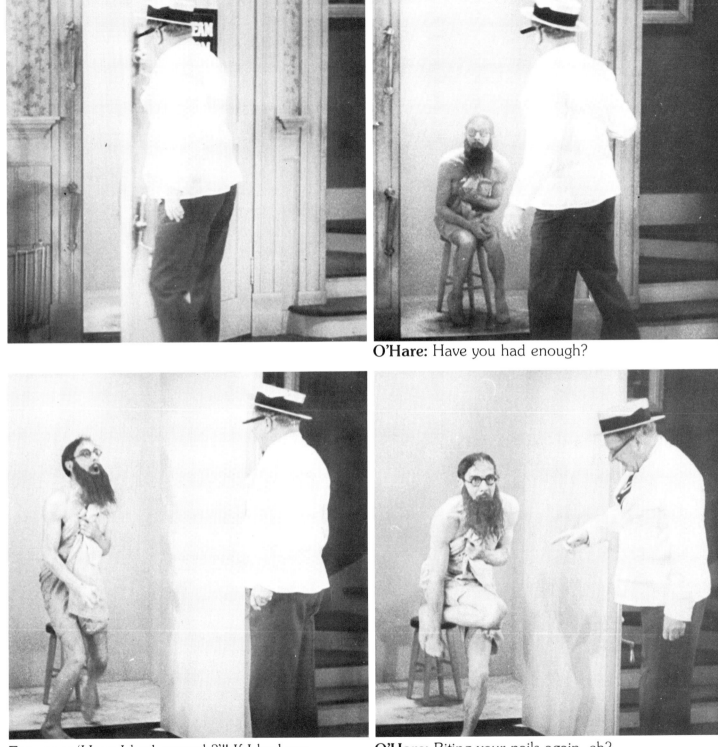

O'Hare: Have you had enough?

Fat man: 'Have I had enough?'!! If I had my former weight, I'd choke you to death. I'll sue you, and take this barber shop away from you.

O'Hare: Biting your nails again, eh?

"And it ain't a fit night out for man or beast."

224